NFTs

by Tiana Laurence
and Seoyoung Kim, PhD

for
dummies
A Wiley Brand

NFTs For Dummies®

Published by: **John Wiley & Sons, Inc.,** 111 River Street, Hoboken, NJ 07030-5774, www.wiley.com

Copyright © 2022 by John Wiley & Sons, Inc., Hoboken, New Jersey

Published simultaneously in Canada

For general information on our other products and services, please contact our Customer Care Department within the U.S. at 877-762-2974, outside the U.S. at 317-572-3993, or fax 317-572-4002. For technical support, please visit https://hub.wiley.com/community/support/dummies.

Wiley publishes in a variety of print and electronic formats and by print-on-demand. Some material included with standard print versions of this book may not be included in e-books or in print-on-demand. If this book refers to media such as a CD or DVD that is not included in the version you purchased, you may download this material at http://booksupport.wiley.com. For more information about Wiley products, visit www.wiley.com.

Library of Congress Control Number: 2021948877

ISBN: 978-1-119-84331-3; 978-1-119-84332-0 (ebk); 978-1-119-84333-7 (ebk)

SKY10030247_110221

Table of Contents

Introduction

Welcome to *NFTs For Dummies!* If you're curious about NFTs — their origin, use cases, and underlying technology — this is the book for you.

In this book, you can find helpful information and advice for exploring the world of NFTs. You can also find useful step-by-step guides that teach you how to set up a hot wallet to store NFTs, how to navigate NFT marketplaces, and even how to code up your very own NFT.

You don't need a background in programming, math, contract theory, or economics to understand this book. We do, however, incorporate these elements to convey a full appreciation of the multidisciplinary nature of NFTs and what they represent.

About This Book

Naturally, this book explains the basics of NFTs, but we also touch on smart contracts and blockchain technology to explain how NFTs are secured and how they operate. Additionally, we touch on various economic and legal themes to convey the rich possibilities of what might be achieved through NFTs.

This book is written to satisfy a diverse array of interests — ranging from lighthearted games to thought leadership in future NFT use cases to more technical explanations that cover the inner workings of the smart contracts that power NFTs and the blockchain technology that secures them.

You don't have to read the book in its entirety to understand the separate topics. This book intends to provide a customizable journey for all audiences — whether you're simply curious to learn the NFT lingo, interested in buying and selling NFTs, or filled with a burning desire to code up and deploy your own ERC-721 non-fungible token.

Foolish Assumptions

The biggest assumption we make about you is that you're interested in learning about NFTs. We mean it!

We do make additional assumptions in writing our how-to guides that are peppered throughout this book. Although we assume no prior knowledge or experience in programming, blockchain technology, or cryptotrading, we do assume that you

>> Have a computer and access to the Internet.

>> Know the basics of navigating your computer and the Internet, and know how to download, install, and run programs.

>> Recognize that some web addresses or long hashes may be split across two lines of text. Keep in mind that these web addresses and large numbers should be copied verbatim as though the line break doesn't exist.

>> Understand that things move quickly, especially in the world of crypto, and that some of our illustrated guides may no longer represent ongoing conditions on the ground by the time you read this book.

Finally, we assume that you know we are not fiduciaries, and we do not provide investment advice. The marketplaces we describe and the step-by-step guides we provide for buying and selling NFTs are meant to be demonstrative and informative.

Icons Used in This Book

Throughout this book, we use the following icons to guide your expectations and direct your attention to certain pieces of information.

TIP

The Tip icon is used to draw your attention to potential shortcuts or easy adaptations that can be made without breaking an entire system. (Yes, you will learn what we mean by this!)

The Remember icon is used to highlight information that's particularly important to know or that can help clear up possible confusion later.

The Technical Stuff icon is used to direct your attention away (if you're a nontechie) or to draw your attention to (if you're an aspiring techie) bits of more technical information that aren't required to understand the main points.

The Warning icon tells you to watch out! It marks important information that may save your time, sanity, tokens, or even friendships.

Beyond the Book

In addition to the material in the print or ebook you're reading right now, this book comes with a free access-anywhere Cheat Sheet with some additional tips for your learning pleasure as well as access to copy-and-paste-able code that should prove helpful in your pursuit to join the nifty world of NFTs. To get this Cheat Sheet, simply go to www.dummies.com and type **NFTs For Dummies Cheat Sheet** in the Search box.

Where to Go from Here

As obvious as this sounds, we recommend that you begin with Chapter 1. From there, you can choose your own adventure based on whether you're more interested in trading, minting, or thinking up imaginative uses of NFTs.

You don't have to read the entire book to understand select topics. We guide you as appropriate if certain sections or chapters require knowledge from an earlier section or chapter in the book.

Let's get started!

1

Getting Started with NFTs

Discover the world of non-fungible tokens.

Meet the very first NFT: *CryptoKitties.*

Find out how to own your own NFTs.

Learn about current and potential uses for NFTs.

Chapter **1**

Introducing Non-Fungible Tokens

t all starts with *Bitcoin:* the original blockchain-based cryptoasset. With the latest run-up in Bitcoin prices (see Figure 1-1), the Internet is buzzing about crypto again. In fact, Google search trends within the US show that Googlers are now as curious about Bitcoin as they are about the country's new president (see Figure 1-2), and interest in NFTs has naturally surged with the Bitcoin tide (see Figure 1-3).

With wild and exciting accounts of art-burning ceremonies and million-dollar NFTs, a mix of amazement, confusion, and even disdain surrounds this mostly "normal" but misunderstood digital creature.

In this chapter, we walk you through the basics of NFTs — what they are, how they work, and what they're used for. The purpose is to provide you with a roadmap to decide which aspects of NFTs you would like to learn more about so that you can customize your reading selections in the chapters that follow.

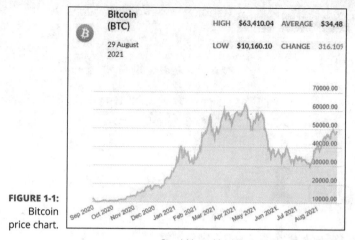

Bitcoin (BTC)

29 August 2021

HIGH $63,410.04 AVERAGE $34,48

LOW $10,160.10 CHANGE 316.109

FIGURE 1-1:
Bitcoin price chart.

From https://coincap.io/assets/bitcoin.

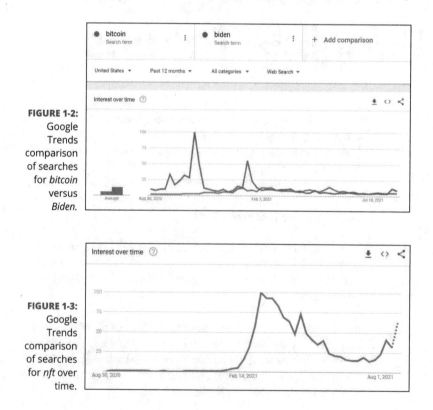

FIGURE 1-2:
Google Trends comparison of searches for *bitcoin* versus *Biden.*

FIGURE 1-3:
Google Trends comparison of searches for *nft* over time.

Beginning at the Beginning: What Is a Non-Fungible Good?

As you've likely learned from friends or Google searches before even purchasing this book, NFT stands for *non-fungible token.* Although tokens themselves are a relatively new development, the idea of grouping fungible and non-fungible goods is not.

Think of dollar bills, shares of Microsoft stock, and Bitcoin — each represent a defined set where items within the set are *fungible.* Put simply, we don't care which dollar bills we receive as long as we receive the right quantity, since each dollar bill fulfills the same purpose and obligations as another.

Non-fungible goods are also a regular and far more prevalent part of our lives. Apples at the grocery store, orchids from the florist, and tickets to an upcoming concert — we inspect our fruit and our flowers to select the ones that are less wilted or bruised. With concerts, each ticket represents a different seat, and a front-row seat is not happily exchanged for a seat that's far removed.

By their nature, non-fungible goods are more difficult to systematically record and track. For one, they require more information to be stored to denote their unique differences. While we can't digitalize the world, there are many instances where we would greatly benefit from a reliable, transparent, and automated system designed to group, organize, and digitally track non-fungible things that are important to us. Here's where NFTs come into play!

REMEMBER

A non-fungible token (NFT) is a unique digital identifier that's secured and stored on a public blockchain. One token is not interchangeable for another, and a token cannot be further divided.

What an NFT actually represents depends on the intent of the developers. Much like how a cryptocurrency — or a fungible token — can represent a global medium of exchange (Bitcoin), a utility token used to fuel smart contracts (Ether), or a financial security linked to shares in a fund (BCAP), NFTs also differ in their current and potential uses.

Although general interest in NFTs has been minimal to nonexistent until recently, the development community has been teeming with fungible token activity for years. Following the successful launchings of Bitcoin (2009), Litecoin (2011), and Dogecoin (2013), a surge of projects followed, each spawning their own fungible tokens. Amidst this crypto-wave, developers began to envision a world of digital collectibles — the crypto-analogue of beanie babies and baseball cards. These projects required a different type of token standard to ensure the uniqueness and non-divisibility of each crypto-baby or crypto-card.

Finally, with the overwhelming success of CryptoKitties, a non-fungible token on Ethereum that debuted in 2017, the ERC-721 Non-Fungible Token Standard soon followed to serve as a blueprint for the development community. (Read more about Crypto-Kitties in Chapter 2.) Since then, there's been an explosion of NFT projects, with more than 15,000 NFTs deployed on Ethereum alone. (See Figure 1-4.)

Non-Fungible Tokens (NFT)			
A total of 15,836 ERC-721 Token Contracts found		First < Page 1 of 317 > Last	
# Token		⌄ Transfers (24H)	Transfers (3D)
1 MutantApeYachtClub The MUTANT APE YACHT CLUB is a collection of up to 20,000 Mutant Apes that can only be created by exposing an existing Bored Ape to a vial of MUTANT SERUM or by minting a Mutant Ape in the public sale.		22,593	22,593
2 Al Cabones (ACBN) The collection consists of 10,000 wanted skeleton mobsters each carrying their own history of ruthless crime.		14,670	18,332
3 Tokenmon		13,828	13,828
4 Hype Hippos		11,185	11,185
5 Drop Bears (DBS) Drop Bears are a collective of 10,000 koalas living on the Ethereum blockchain.		10,925	10,926

FIGURE 1-4: The five most active NFTs.

Exploring Uses for NFTs

The NFT space is still in its infancy, but already the development community is teeming with ideas on how to put them to good use. The most natural use case — the one currently dominating the marketplace — is in tracking digital collectibles. From there, gaming items and digital media were natural extensions.

However, despite the recent explosion of NFTs, the current implementations are still rather limited in their scope, and mostly surround monetization of collectibles. The industry has also been hampered by the get-rich-quick mentality that has plagued crypto-space in general and has also attracted many unscrupulous players.

Still, we see many interesting use cases for NFTs on the horizon. Some of these could truly disrupt the way we validate, track, and assign ownership of unique and esoteric items or work to effectively democratize content creation and distribution. Imagine taking the costly detective work out of verifying the ownership history of a rare collectible. Or imagine a world where expensive eBay auctions include proof of ownership on the Ethereum blockchain. Much attention is centered on speculation right now, but the potential value added by these exciting possibilities far overshadow the headlines announcing the latest NFT millionaires and NFT scam artists.

The cryptocurrency world was also met with a similar breadth of reactions, ranging from deep skepticism to enthusiastic acceptance. But as governments and major financial institutions began to accept Bitcoin and Ether, the promise of the underlying technology came to the forefront of discussions. Although NFTs have the benefit of following their crypto-frontrunners (who themselves are still quite young), we need much more time to see how the NFT ecosystem will evolve and what it will spawn next.

Finding Out How an NFT Works

People often confuse the NFT itself with what the NFT was built to represent. An *NFT* is a cryptographically secure digital record that verifies your ownership of or access to, say, a piece of digital art — sort of like how your car title verifies ownership of your vehicle. You don't really own the car in your possession without the title, and you don't really own the CryptoKitty in your collection of jpegs without the corresponding NFT.

For example, consider the cryptocollectible known as Mutant Ape Yacht Club (MAYC). This strange new collection of mutant apes (who may or may not be part of a yacht club?) is the latest rage among NFT collectors and is now the most active ERC-721 token out there. (See Figure 1-5.) But what exactly does it mean to own a particular MAYC?

FIGURE 1-5: MAYCs listed for public sale on OpenSea.

When browsing MAYCs for sale on OpenSea (one of the NFT marketplaces you can discover in Chapter 4 and Chapter 12), you notice provocative graphics and characteristics presented on the marketplace platform. (Refer to Figure 1-5.) What you're seeing are the visual representations of each individual MAYC — but the NFT itself is the unique digital code that's secured on the Ethereum blockchain.

For instance, consider MAYC #7632 in the upper left corner of Figure 1-5. Purchasing this NFT means that you're now the rightful owner of record of TokenID 7632, which is in storage in the contract account `0x60e4d786628fea6478f785` `a6d7e704777c86a7c6` on the Ethereum blockchain. All transfers of ownership will be memorialized on the blockchain so that provenance of MAYC #7632 and its current rightful owner can always be known, as shown in Figure 1-6.

A collectible   The associated ID

FIGURE 1-6:
MAYC
#7632.

As of this writing, 14,688 MAYCs exist across 7,709 holders. You can check out the individual details and ownership of each unique MAYC at `https://etherscan.io/token/0x60e4d786628fea6478 f785a6d7e704777c86a7c6.`

REMEMBER

The digital art you purchase is easy to duplicate. (Pressing the PrintScreen key on the keyboard requires little to no training.) However, because the NFT is secured on a public blockchain, it's far more difficult to illegally transfer, duplicate, or otherwise hack. The beauty of NFTs lies in the underlying technology — a nexus of smart contracts and distributed network of validators — that allows you to reliably and automatically verify who truly owns each of the 14,688 mutant ape NFTs.

Thus, our mutant apes are part of a greater decentralized ecosystem where records are kept in a public and trustless manner, which means that we don't need a trusted central party, such as Bank of America, to maintain a reliable and secure system to track our mutant apes for us. In their peculiar way, these mutant apes are bringing further awareness to the burgeoning landscape of decentralized finance (DeFi) and decentralized autonomous organizations (DAOs). (To read more about DAOs, check out Chapters 4 and 6.)

The majority of NFTs are minted as ERC-721 tokens on Ethereum. Thus, as shown in Figure 1-6, the provenance of each token is memorialized on the public Ethereum blockchain. Each subsequent transaction is validated and executed by a distributed network of miners — much like the system securing the Bitcoin blockchain.

TECHNICAL STUFF

Because an NFT is secured on a robust and tested blockchain (to date, the Ethereum blockchain has never been hacked), developers of nascent projects can piggyback off the existing system in place to secure ownership records and reward systems within the latest sub-economy under development. We caution though, that, although the Ethereum blockchain itself has yet to be hacked, individual smart contracts deployed on Ethereum have. Thus, the recommended practice is to use vetted libraries that provide pre-built smart contracts implementing development standards that have been reviewed and finalized by the greater community of core developers.

We promise that the preceding paragraph makes much more sense after you dive into the technical chapters in Part 3 of this book.

Buying NFTs

If you're curious how to buy an NFT, you should know that it's quite easy. There are now many marketplaces where you can purchase NFTs, and OpenSea is just one of many venues. Starting with Chapter 2, we walk you through how to set up a wallet to hold your NFTs and how to purchase your first NFT.

If your heart is set on learning more details, jump to Chapters 4 and 5, which acquaint you with the practical considerations of buying (and selling) NFTs, and see Chapter 12 for a guide to ten NFT marketplaces.

Before you jump ahead, though, we have two main considerations that we'd like to highlight.

Why buy NFTs

First, should you buy NFTs? Maybe. It depends on your motivations.

If you plan to actually *use* the NFT, then yes — you should buy it! For instance, perhaps the NFT provides you entry to a venue or gives you the legal right to post certain digital media on your website. In these cases, your only legitimate course of action would be to purchase the NFT.

We also advocate checking out NFT marketplaces for educational or even entertainment purposes. Perhaps you simply want to know how to go through the motions of buying an NFT. Or, perhaps you're more likely to learn the underlying technology and explore additional use cases if you begin by purchasing an NFT.

In any of these circumstances, the biggest question is, "Are you spending money that you would seriously regret losing?" If so, then you certainly should not buy NFTs.

NFTs as investments

We think of investments from the lens of traditional investment management principles. The gist is that you should be well-diversified and rebalance over time so that you bear less risk as you approach retirement.

We don't advocate individual stock-picking as a sound investment practice, and neither do we advocate NFT-picking as an investment practice. But, as we mention earlier, we aren't opposed to setting aside money that you *won't miss*, in order to have a little fun. This fun might mean a trip to Mexico, a dinner at Napa Valley's swanky French Laundry restaurant, or mutant ape NFTs.

Of course, as the NFT asset class matures, you develop a better sense of the risk-return trade-off of various NFTs and their appropriate allocations, if any, within a well-diversified investment portfolio. After all, with Bitcoin now approaching a $1 trillion dollar market cap, we all should consider allocating a (tiny) portion of any truly broadly diversified portfolio to Bitcoin. Of course, this is a far cry from putting relatively large amounts of money in individual "investments" — whether it's individual stocks or NFTs or Beanie Babies — in the hope of hitting the jackpot.

Proceeding on Your NFT Journey

First and foremost, we hope this book is an enjoyable way for you to learn more about this emerging asset class. Beyond that, we hope to spark creative energy, encourage new implementations, and dissuade you from succumbing to the desire for making a quick buck.

We wish you a fulfilling journey as you go on to select your next chapter. Cheers!

Chapter **2**

Owning Your Own NFT

I n this chapter, you dive into the exciting world of non-fungible tokens (NFTs), which is taking place inside Dapper Labs' CryptoKitty platform. Playing *CryptoKitties* can help you gain a deep understanding of how NFTs are created and traded.

We show you how to set up an NFT wallet and an exchange so that you can buy and (eventually create and) sell your first NFT and explore with confidence the new markets as well as the changing business models NFTs have introduced.

Dapper Labs is working hard to make its platforms accessible to everyone, no matter their technical background. This chapter also prepares you to access other NFT marketplaces, which we cover in Part 2 of this book.

Where It All Began: Non-Fungible Kitties

NFTs can credit their existence to *CryptoKitties* (www. cryptokitties.com), a novel game that was launched in the fall of 2017, by Dapper Labs. (Dapper Labs also created the smash hit *Top Shop*, the platform that allowed users to purchase NFTs of their favorite NBA players.) The creators felt that the general population didn't understand what a cryptocurrency was or why it mattered, let alone how its technology worked. Likewise, the public perception of blockchain applications remained narrow-minded and focused on get-rich-quick scams, dark web utility, and new financial instruments. The creators wanted to change the shortsighted perception in the market and demystify its potential and long-term implications, which had remained esoteric at best.

Blockchain for the masses

CryptoKitties provided a new angle from which the general public could view blockchain. As one of the world's first blockchain games, *CryptoKitties* could take advantage of all the same blockchain technology that makes Bitcoin possible. *CryptoKitties* isn't a digital currency; it's a *cryptocollectible* (a unique, non-fungible digital asset), and it has the same security as a cryptocurrency.

Each CryptoKitty (see Figure 2-1) is one-of-a-kind and cannot be replicated, removed, or destroyed. Playing the game sometimes requires a significant amount of resources, but a user gains an intimate understanding of how cryptocurrencies and blockchains work while having fun. (The game is a tad addictive, to say the least.)

FIGURE 2-1:
Learn about crypto currency while buying and selling cute cats.

CryptoKitties not only introduced the world to NFTs but also introduced NFTs that could make their own NFTs. They took the more-difficult-to-understand features of blockchains — like its implications for digital permanence and the traceable provenance of data that can't be faked — and built them into their game mechanics.

Dapper Labs also understood the limitations of earlier blockchain projects. Many blockchain solutions were looking for problems and had to use one-time fundraising events for cryptocurrencies, called initial coin offerings (ICOs). *CryptoKitties* was one of the few blockchain projects in 2017 that didn't host an ICO. But they were so popular that the sale of kitties broke their blockchain, slowing the transaction speeds for the rest of the users — a limitation Dapper Labs may have overlooked.

The sales of these unique digital cats, secured by way of the new token called ERC 721, slowed Ethereum to a crawl. The systems struggled to keep up with the demand for these cute little cats.

The Ethereum was a new blockchain that was designed with internal programing languages that allows developers to build *blockchain applications* — ones that could take advantage of distributed networks and built-in systems for clearing and settling transactions. Tokens were the killer app for blockchains, allowing almost anyone to issue a whole range of rare digital item — equities, currencies, coupons, and more.

ERC 721 added to the functionality of the earlier tokens by introducing an open standard that describes how to build non-fungible or unique tokens on the Ethereum blockchain. The Kitties perfectly demonstrated the functionality and limitations of blockchain technology while also making it fun and approachable.

The game made waves all over the world, even in mainstream media outlets like the *New York Times*, *Wired*, *Forbes*, *CNN Money*, and many more. It was fascinating to see this quirky and well-designed game change blockchain forever.

The CryptoKitty development team built a sustainable revenue-based model that allows them to keep growing as they acquire new users. Before *CryptoKitties*, blockchain struggled with sustainable business models. Often, the token economics didn't align with user interest and market demand. *CryptoKitties* showed the world that blockchain technologies could be used for anything — even silly and cute games that let you breed digital cats.

Not just a passing fad

Skeptics who thought cryptogames were just a passing fad for bored millennials have been proven wrong. *CryptoKitties,* which proved that anything can generate value on top of blockchains if it has sufficient token economics, allows users to access block-chain technology in a way that users find engaging. The token economics are solid, and the utility is apparent to anyone. Most importantly, users didn't have to open their terminals or know how to code. They could just play.

REMEMBER

Distributed ledger technology (I tell you more about this topic in the next section) that supports non-fungible tokens has the potential to turn into the biggest revolution of the information age. Its potential applications are varied beyond just digital cats, even if that's where it began for NFTs.

The impact of NFTs

Since the inception of blockchain in 2009, it has been disrupting numerous industries. However, the general concept of blockchain technology, especially in the mind of the mass consumer, was still beyond most people's comprehension. (The Internet, in its early days, also seemed like an unfathomable mystery to most people.)

Democratizing blockchain

NFTs democratized blockchain, making it accessible and extremely valuable to a wide variety of people. NFTs took a once costly and time-consuming activity — selling a collector's item — and made it instantaneous and verifiable, similarly to how email was a paradigm shift for sending a letter, which could take days or weeks to arrive at its destination. With email, you could instantaneously receive or send a written message any-where in the world. NFTs are the same for ownership of unique digital items and, maybe someday in the future, they can represent tangible assets.

TECHNICAL STUFF

Blockchain is the underlying technology that powers NFTs. (You've probably heard about blockchain in passing, but you might not be aware of many of its aspects.) Blockchain is a *distributed ledger* system where information can securely and reliably be stored and where any modification of this stored information is governed by strict rules. For example, no single party can change data without the whole system being made aware of it. (You might not think that's an interesting strategy, but data before blockchain was secured by an admin who had godlike powers over the records.)

NFTs derive their value from being trustworthy records of provenance. You can record transactions between yourself and another party efficiently and verifiably on the system's blockchain. The record of the transfer of your NFT becomes an immutable shared memory, distributed across the world with strict built-in accountability features.

Representing ownership

NFTs can represent ownership of all sorts of items, including digital artworks and in-game elements, not just digital cats. These NFTs are typically purchased for Ethereum or Bitcoin on a *centralized exchange* — a platform (like the NBA Top Shop) that facilitates the transaction.

Trading between users

NFTs can be traded on a peer-to-peer basis without the need for an intermediary. In this model, the trade takes place directly between two people or groups instead of using one person (or company) as an intermediary for all trades to facilitate and monitor them. This means there's no need to rely on another party, like eBay or Amazon, to buy something from someone else; you can do it yourself using just your phone.

The internal exchange mechanisms that allow users to trade between themselves without an intermediary are called *decentralized exchanges* (DEXes), which enable you to sell your assets independently of a third party — they're becoming popular because centralized exchanges are vulnerable to theft. Exchanges run by a company require the system to be controlled by a single party, negating the power of blockchain and turning it against the user. If an item is stolen from a company exchange, it's nearly impossible to retrieve it again.

Enabling smart contracts

NFTs enable decentralized exchanges via *smart contracts* — computer scripts that run on those ledger nodes with access to data about the NFT. For example, when you purchase a Crypto-Kitty, you purchase a piece of unique digital art that has been coded with ownership that automatically changes when payment is made — all without the need for a third-party agent. This system reduces risk while expediting transactions by eliminating intermediaries. Similar to the email example we mention earlier, exchanging ownership instantaneously with anyone in the world is now possible.

Creating digital scarcity

The *CryptoKitties* team addressed the concept of digital scarcity for singular items by way of their digital collectibles. No two Crypto-Kitties are alike — each one is unique. Digital goods, which aren't a new concept, have seen real-world valuation. For example, *World of Warcraft*'s gold farmers use the Steam platform's online marketplace, where users can buy and sell in-game items across their PC's video game collection. However, this niche, which was limited to video games, lacked the features that blockchain affords. You can find numerous examples of hacking or cheating or developers influencing the ecosystem.

Digital collectibles hold immense potential that started with digital cats but has since moved on to all types of collectibles and art.

Solving problems

Adding NFT to the mix has changed how people perceive digital collectibles, as evidenced by the intense interest shown in digital collectibles such as CryptoPunks and other NFTs. A digital art enthusiast paid a whopping $69.3 million for the NFT named *EVERYDAYS: THE FIRST 5000 DAYS*. The *Genesis* CryptoKitty NFT, the rarest in existence, sold for 246.926 Ether.

The size, scope, and long-term pedigree of these NFTs alleviate fears associated with cryptocurrencies, as the following list makes clear:

>> **The central issuing authority problem:** When digital collectibles are created and issued and the market identifies the rarest or the most popular collectibles, nothing stops the creator from simply creating more. When this happens, it diminishes the value of the original collectibles, potentially making them worthless.

>> **The provider dependency problem:** The existence of a digital collectible is dependent on the presence of the issuing authority. If a digital collectible is created and the initial creator ceases to exist, your digital collectibles also cease to exist. NFTs, on the other hand, live on distributed ledgers that replicate. If the token economics of the blockchain are in line with the network's nodes, your NFT is safe. Most NFTs just contain the smart contract, which in many cases points to a URL (huge risk, since the host could be shut down or the content changes on their end). The image might be too large or it might simply be too tedious to integrate.

>> **Purpose and function of digital collectibles:** Physical collectibles are popular because of their intended purpose. If you collect art, for example, it can be worth a lot of money, and it serves a purpose by hanging on your wall as an item of beauty and status.

With the help of blockchain technologies, these problems have been solved, which has made people far more willing to invest in digital collectibles outside the niche of video games. If NFT digital collectibles hold their value the same way a physical collectible does, an entirely new world of collecting will come to life.

The game mechanics of CryptoKitties

Dapper Labs' CryptoKitties are digital, collectible cats built on the Ethereum blockchain. They can be bought and sold using *ether*, the native cryptocurrency of Ethereum. You can breed your cats to create new cats with exciting traits and varying levels of cuteness.

At the launch in 2017, 50,000 Gen 0 cats, known as Clock Cats, were created with a smart contract on the Ethereum blockchain. (Gen 0 means that they were the first cats created.) Existing as programs stored on a blockchain, *smart contracts* have preset conditions and the terms of a contract between the buyer and seller written directly in the code. For more on smart contracts, see Chapter 9. Clock Cats were distributed automatically via smart contract at a rate of one cat every 15 minutes. Each cat was sold at auction.

A CryptoKitty is unique in appearance, with distinct features. Its phenotype is determined by its immutable genes (genotype) stored in the smart contract. In fact, all the fundamental game mechanics of *CryptoKitties* are tied to smart contracts. By gamifying blockchain technology, the *CryptoKitties* team normalized previously esoteric concepts and empowered users with essential fluency in blockchain technology. Now you get the chance to gain the same knowledge.

By giving you the ability to breed your very own cats, the kitties became more than just a digital collectible. They are personal. [See the later section "Collecting, Breeding, and Selling Your Very Own Non-Fungible (Crypto)Kitties," to learn more about these fun digital felines.] The *CryptoKitties* team also creates a self-sustaining community where users can create new collectibles and trade them on the Ethereum blockchain.

What's In Your Wallet? Setting Up MetaMask

MetaMask is a free browser extension and smartphone app that allows you to interact with the Ethereum blockchain. It lets you log in to dApp websites with your wallet keys and send and receive coins from your cryptocurrency wallet. To learn about other wallets and decide which is the best for you, see Chapter 4.

To set up a MetaMask wallet, follow these steps:

1. **Navigate to the MetaMask website at** `https://metamask.io`.

You can see the support that MetaMask gives you. It works on Chrome, Firefox, Brave, and Edge browsers. At the time of writing, it doesn't support Safari, but it does offer an iPhone app as well as an Android app. We're using Chrome for this example.

2. **Click the Download Now button and then click Install MetaMask for Chrome.**

3. **At the Chrome web store, click Add to Chrome.**

   When your browser is done downloading MetaMask, you see the option to either import an existing wallet or set up a new MetaMask wallet.

4. **Click the Add a New Wallet link.**

   MetaMask asks you to send some data to them. It won't reveal your identity, but it's used to make the service better. You can opt out if you want to.

5. **Create a password.**

   This is a password just for MetaMask. It isn't the recovery phrase or the private keys for your wallet. The password is secondary security.

   You're taken to the security-phrase screen, where it prompts you to write down a recovery phrase. Do *not* skip this section.

6. **Write down the words clearly, and store the paper in a safe place.**

   You may want to go so far as laminating your paper and storing it in a vault. You need the recovery phrase if you lose your password or device.

7. **On the next screen, confirm the recovery phrase so that MetaMask knows that you wrote it down properly.**

   After you have correctly entered the recovery phrase, you can get into your MetaMask wallet.

TIP

The MetaMask team is always making updates. Check back frequently to see what they have added.

8. **Within your wallet Navigate to Settings and click the General tab to change your currency conversion and choose the primary currency.**

This is how all the holdings in your MetaMask wallet are valued.

9. **Choose a language.**

If you navigate to the Advanced section, you can reset the account and clear your entire transaction history. You can also find some other controls, including advanced gas controls.

10. **Navigate to the main page and click the three dots on the right side of your wallet.**

There you can see your account details, including your Ethereum address. You need your Ethereum address to receive Ethereum-based tokens. This is as simple as scanning the QR code with your smartphone. If you already have a crypto-exchange app, you can skip the "Setting Up Coinbase" section bellow.

REMEMBER

A *cryptocurrency wallet,* like MetaMask and others, allows you to store cryptocurrency, like Ether (ETH). You need to use an *exchange platform,* like Coinbase.com, to convert US dollars (or any real-world currency) to cryptocurrency that you then store in your wallet. Exchange services often provide a wallet, but you can use any wallet with any exchange. The Coinbase Wallet, for instance, is a separate app available to use with a Coinbase.com account. However, you don't have to have a Coinbase.com account to use the Coinbase wallet, and vice versa.

Setting Up Coinbase

Coinbase.com is a popular exchange service that allows you to connect your bank account to a cryptowallet and purchase from an ever-growing list of assets.

TIP

You must be at least 18 years old and have a government-issued photo ID to set up Coinbase. Passport cards are not accepted. You also need a computer or smartphone connected to the Internet. Coinbase verifies your phone number via text messages.

Creating your Coinbase account

Coinbase charges no fee to create or maintain your account but does charge transaction fees. Follow these steps to create your Coinbase account:

1. **Go to** www.coinbase.com **from a browser on your computer, or download and open the Coinbase app on an Android or iOS phone.**

2. **Click or tap Get Started.**

3. **Enter your legal name, your email address, and a password.**

   Make sure to write down your password and the seed phrase that's generated for you, and store both in a secure place. (The *seed phrase* is a random set of words that are used to recover your wallet. Think of them as a special password.)

4. **Provide your state of residence.**

5. **Select the check box and click Create Account from a computer, or tap Sign Up from a mobile phone.**

   Coinbase sends a verification email to your email address.

6. **Navigate to the email and select Verify Email Address to verify your Coinbase account.**

   Make sure the email came from no–reply@coinbase.com.

   You're taken back to Coinbase.com.

7. **Sign in using the email and password you created initially to complete the email verification process.**

Verifying your phone number

After you've created the Coinbase account and verified your email address, you need to verify your phone number, too. Just follow these steps:

1. **Sign in to Coinbase.**

2. **When prompted, select your country and add the mobile phone number.**

3. **Click the Send Code popup from a computer or tap Continue on your mobile phone.**

4. **Enter the 7-digit code that Coinbase texts to your phone number and then click Submit (from your computer) or Continue (from your phone).**

Adding your personal information

You add the information shown on your valid government–issued photo ID, so have it handy when you complete these steps:

1. **Stay in your Coinbase app.**

   After verifying your phone number, Coinbase asks you to submit a photo of your ID.

2. **Enter your first name, last name, date of birth, and address, and answer the following questions:**

   - What do you use Coinbase for?
   - What is your source of funds?
   - What is your current occupation?
   - Who is your employer?
   - What are the last four digits of your social security number (SSN)?

3. **Click Continue to finish the process.**

This step completes the application process. You need to wait until you receive further instructions via email to know that your account is approved. At that point, you can complete the next section.

Verifying your identity and adding your bank account

When you receive the additional instructions mentioned in the previous section, do the following:

1. **Sign in to your Coinbase account.**

2. **Complete the ID verification process.**

Set up 2-step verification, such as a time-based one-time password (TOTP) to help protect against unauthorized account access. Google offers one called Authenticator, which you can find on the Apple App Store or the Google Play Store.

Adding funds to your wallet

If you haven't already done so, send some ETH to your MetaMask wallet. Just sign in to your wallet and follow these steps:

1. **On the main page of your wallet, click the Buy button.**

   From there, you have the choice to add tokens via a wallet you already have or by using Wyre.

2. **Select Directly Deposit Ether and copy your MetaMask wallet address.**

3. **Navigate back to your Coinbase wallet and use it to send yourself enough ETH to buy a CryptoKitty and cover the fees for the exchange.**

   The price of processing your purchase changes daily — review the fee before processing the transaction.

4. **With funds in your MetaMask wallet, you can navigate back to the *CryptoKitties* website at** www.cryptokitties. com **to purchase your first kitty.**

If you need additional help setting up a wallet or an exchange app, check out *Blockchain For Dummies*, 2nd Edition, by Tiana Laurence, or *Ethereum For Dummies*, by Michael G. Solomon. Both books cover this topic in greater detail.

Collecting, Breeding, and Selling Your Very Own Non-Fungible (Crypto)Kitties

The *CryptoKitties* game has four main functions: buying, breeding, siring, and trading. Buying is a straightforward process where you buy an NFT of a digital cat.

Once you own the NFT of the cat, you can then create a new NFT by breeding your own CryptoKitty. You also have the ability to lease out your CryptoKitty to be used as a "sire" to other users who want to breed their CryptoKitties. The Offer feature allows users to bid on cats that aren't for sale, and you can trade one cat for another with anyone who's willing to make the trade.

Buying your first CryptoKitty

The buying function is straightforward. After you have your MetaMask set up (see the steps in the earlier section "What's In Your Wallet? Setting Up MetaMask"), you can head to the marketplace to find yourself a cute little kitty.

You can start by looking around on the *CryptoKitties* marketplace to find some CryptoKitties. They aren't free (unless someone gives you one, a transaction that still requires that you have a wallet) and can cost between $3 and $100,000 — but you pay for them using ETH in your wallet.

To find a CryptoKitty and buy it, follow these steps:

1. **Navigate to** www.cryptokitties.co/search.

2. **Browse the Kitties on the page, enter search terms at the top, or choose Kitty Type, Generation, and Cooldown.**

3. **Click Next at the bottom to see more pages of Kitties.**

4. **When you find a Kitty you'd like to buy, click the Buy Now button.**

   A new page opens.

5. **Double-click the Kitty you're about to purchase.**

6. **If everything seems in order, click the OK, Buy This Kitty button.**

You're prompted with a Dapper Labs transaction window. It asks you to set up a wallet (if you don't have one) at www.meetdapper.com. If you decided not to get a MetaMask wallet, follow the instructions on the Dapper Labs page, and then return to ordering your Kitty.

7. **Click the Submit button to purchase the Kitty.**

After you purchase a Kitty, it may take a couple of minutes to show up on your profile. The Ethereum blockchain needs to record the transaction and update the blockchain with your new ownership transfer, which all depends on the Ethereum network.

Using the Offer function

Offers are another way to buy cats. Using the game's Offers system, players can make a bid in ETH for any Kitty they want that isn't already up for sale. After an offer is made, the owner has three days to accept or decline before the offer expires.

Breeding your kitties

In *CryptoKitties*, you can breed to produce a new cat that is the genetic combination of its parents. If you have plans to breed a cat you want to buy, be sure to look at its pedigree. Anticipating the outcome is unknown, and the possibilities for unique and rare genetic makeups of a CryptoKitty are endless. Each cat has unique *Cattributes* that are visible, but certain traits can be unlocked by way of breeding. Knowing the breeding cats' Cattributes can help you determine the likely outcomes of breeding.

One cat acts as the sire in each breeding pair and will have a recovery period before breeding again. The second cat, the dame, incubates the kitten, during which time it cannot engage in another pairing. You can breed your Kitties in two ways:

>> Breed two of your own cats.

>> Breed one of your cats with a public sire or dame. If your cat is the sire, you're paid a fee by the dame's owner.

REMEMBER

Fees are involved with breeding, even if you're breeding two of your own cats: 0.015 ETH at the time of writing but this changes with market conditions.

Though a CryptoKitty can breed any number of times, the recovery and gestational periods increase the more they mate, so pay attention to the breed time (next to the Clock icon underneath your Kitty's picture). The more times your prospective cat has been used to breed, the slower it is to produce offspring.

Breed two kitties of the same generation. The kitten they produce is given a generation number that's the highest generation of both parents plus one. For example, if you breed a Gen 4 Kitty with a Gen 5 Kitty, you get a Gen 6 cat. If you breed two Gen 10s, on the other hand, you get a Gen 11.

Chapter **3**

The Future of NFTs

I f you happen to be reading this book chronologically, by now you have a sense of what NFTs are (defined in Chapter 1) and perhaps have even purchased one (you can see how in Chapter 2). But between the cuteness of the *CryptoKitties* and the glamor of $69 million NFTs, the actual essence of NFTs can easily be forgotten. A *non-fungible token (NFT)* is simply a cryptographically secure digital code that verifies ownership of non-fungible (that is, unique) items.

This chapter covers the future potential of NFTs and what NFTs could mean for property rights. Before we jump into those topics, however, we first give you some insight into the infamous NFT fetching $69,346,250 at Christie's by taking a look under the hood at the actual internal workings of this prohibitively expensive NFT. What exactly is this Beeple NFT, if it's not the artwork itself?

Dissecting the Anatomy of a $69 Million NFT

The artist known as Beeple began his *EVERYDAYS* collection with the commitment to create a new digital piece of art every day for 5,000 days. The famed piece in question, *EVERYDAYS — THE FIRST*

5000 DAYS, marks the conclusion of this artistic journey, which began in May 2007 and culminated in the minting of the corresponding NFT on February 16, 2021. The final *EVERYDAYS* piece itself is shown in Figure 3-1, but what was Beeple actually selling?

25 Feb - 11 Mar 2021 | Online Auction 20447
Beeple | The First 5000 Days   Lot 1

Beeple (b. 1981)
EVERYDAYS: THE FIRST 5000 DAYS

Price Realised   Estimate
USD   unknown
69,346,250

Closed: **11 Mar 2021**

♡ Save   ⬆ Share

FIGURE 3-1: Beeple's famed digital artwork, *EVERYDAYS — THE FIRST 5000 DAYS.*

Since digital images are a matrix of pixel values, Beeple boiled down his approximately 300-megabyte creation to a numerical condensation (known as a *hash code*) of the machine-level representation of the graphic. This hash code was then included with additional metadata, hashed again, and stored as part of the Beeple NFT's metadata alongside the tokenURI, `ipfs://ipfs/QmPAg1mjxcEQPPtqsLoEcauVedaeMH81WXDPvPx3VC5zUz`, providing a roadmap to find Beeple's *EVERYDAYS — THE FIRST 5000 DAYS* digital artwork on the IPFS peer-to-peer network. And thus, Beeple's digital art was disseminated, and `token ID 49013` (in smart contract address: `0x2a46f2ffd99e19a89476 e2f62270e0a35bbf0756`) was born! (For more on the IPFS network, check out the nearby sidebar, "Diving into the dark web.")

These details appear within the event logs of the transaction in which Beeple minted his $69 million NFT, as shown in Figure 3-2. The corresponding identifying details of this NFT are on the Christie's auction site, as shown in Figure 3-3. (If you're curious, you can view the full transaction details here: `https://etherscan.io/tx/0x84760768c527794ede901f97973385bfc1b f2e297f7ed16f523f75412ae772b3`.)

DIVING INTO THE DARK WEB

IPFS stands for the *InterPlanetary File System*, which is part of what's colloquially called the dark web or darknet. IPFS is a decentralized file-sharing network based on content-addressable storage, which allows data to be accessed based on its content rather than solely on where it's stored. The QmPAg1mjxcEQPPtqsLoEcau VedaeMH81WXDPvPx3VC5zUz portion of the tokenURI provides the content metadata, which IPFS needs in order to identify files across the distributed network. Yes, Beeple has freely distributed his actual digital artwork via the modern-day version of Napster!

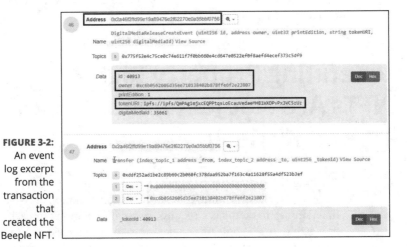

FIGURE 3-2:
An event log excerpt from the transaction that created the Beeple NFT.

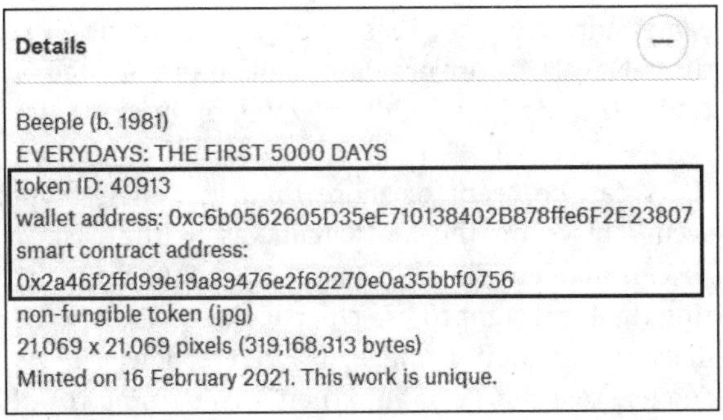

FIGURE 3-3:
Details of the Beeple NFT from Christie's online auction site.

In the end, what did the auction winner actually purchase? In this particular case, the NFT doesn't confer exclusive, legal access rights to the digital art (the digital art itself has been freely distributed as a public good); nor does it represent claims to royalty income from its use. What we have is an incredible piece of financial technology (FinTech) history — we have a disintermediated-yet-secure ownership record memorialized on the Ethereum blockchain, and we can now reliably trace the history of this unique digital item to verify who owns it now and who has owned it in the past.

By bringing awareness to this promising technology, Beeple and his highest bidder are providing a basis for the future of NFTs. You can read more in Chapter 13 about *THE FIRST 5000 DAYS*, and about nine other NFTs that sold for incredible prices (including two more of Beeple's artwork).

Redefining Property Rights (NFTs Are Not Just about Digital Art and Kitties!)

Tracking the ownership and lineage of *CryptoKitties* (or Beeple's NFT) is just the beginning of what NFTs can accomplish. Well-functioning marketplaces require well-defined and enforceable property rights. People often take for granted the trusted intermediaries who serve this important purpose — for example, they rely on the county clerk to maintain records of property ownership, and they trust the DMV to maintain records of car titles. Now NFTs are providing a disintermediated way to memorialize transactions and verify ownership.

NFTs can be seen for more than just their cryptographically secure place on the blockchain, as in the case of the Beeple NFT. In modern times, transferring ownership entails transferring the legal right to use a particular asset, whether it's a car, a house, or a digital image. ("Finders, keepers" is not a legal defense to a charge of auto theft.) This framework fits well with NFTs, which can be created to legally represent titles, deeds, or licenses.

Overall, NFTs have the potential to reliably trace peer-to-peer transfers of ownership records without the need for a trusted third-party to verify the integrity of these transactions. Their ability to instantaneously track and validate the ownership of each unique item makes them particularly suited to disrupt any marketplace where verifying the provenance of a unique item is faulty or inadequate.

NFTs and Digital Property

Tracking digital property was a natural starting point for NFTs. From digital collectibles to gaming items and digital media, NFTs have the potential to truly democratize the creator economy.

Music, movies, and books

Until recently, consumers have had to own music in order to hear it on demand. From records to cassette tapes and from CDs to mp3s, ownership of the physical or digital media was taken for granted as the status quo.

Despite the convenience of digital music, it felt comforting to buy and sell physical media — artists knew that only one instance could play at a time and, once passed on, consumers no longer had access. Thus, the first-sale doctrine was enacted to establish that physical copies can be resold by the purchaser without permission from the copyright holder of the work itself.

Now, it seems that owned music has become a thing of the past — with streaming services far surpassing the purchasing and downloading of music. This situation was only natural, given that digital copies don't degrade in quality and, accordingly, the US Copyright Office has been hesitant to apply the first-sale doctrine to digital transmissions. Anyone can easily sell the digital music they purchased while retaining a copy on their personal devices.

If the true ownership and access rights of digital media are well established and easily verified, sales and transfers in the digital sphere should be no different from sales and transfers in the physical domain. Thus, NFTs could bring back the concept of owned media (and the first-sale doctrine!) in the digital era, to not only music but also movies and books.

Photos and other digital art

The market for digital images also provides a natural habitat for NFTs, which can be used to reliably demonstrate the legal right to a particular digital photo or artwork. Imagine creating an NFT alongside a digital image you own (which can include the NFT's identifying information in its image metadata) to record its rightful owner and permissioned users. The potential economic advantages to digital artists and photographers, who typically serve as contributors to Shutterstock and Getty Images, is huge.

With the increasing accuracy of image search engines (see Figure 3-4), content creators can locate and cross-check unauthorized users of their digital content in an automated fashion, and authorized users can validate their legal claim by using the corresponding NFT and image metadata.

FIGURE 3-4: A sample image search on Google.

A public figure may also use NFTs to mitigate the creation of a *deepfake* (a video or an image with a person's likeness added or replaced with the use of deep learning technology). Imagine Obama NFTs, where a new token is created for each legitimate piece of digital Obama media. Consumers can verify whether an image, an audio file, or a video has been altered by checking its hash against the varying Obama media tokens. Of course, in a trust-based state, you could rely on central authorities to publish a list of valid media hashes. But in unstable regimes, an immutable and disintermediated account of valid content hashes is integral to ensuring that the public can believe what they see.

Game assets

With the popularity of online role-playing games like *EverQuest* and *League of Legends,* assets within the game began to fetch real-world dollars from gamers who were eager to accrue in-game wealth more rapidly or to achieve status by flexing a unique item within the game.

Gamers list their assets on marketplaces such as eBay or Player-Auctions (see Figure 3-5) with the promise to transfer the asset within the game after payment (a process inherently fraught with risk). NFTs provide a natural way to reliably represent ownership of game assets and avatars and to facilitate automatic peer-to-peer transfers via smart contracts. Imagine a gaming world with truly democratized ownership and exchange of assets — experienced gamers keep a greater portion of their sales revenue, novice gamers pay less for gaming street cred, and the peer-to-peer exchanges are instantaneous and virtually risk free.

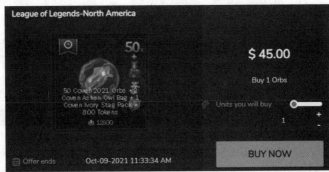

FIGURE 3-5:
A *League of Legends* in-game asset for sale on Player Auctions.

NFTs and Real Property

Many instances in the physical world would also greatly benefit from a reliable, transparent, and automated system designed to group, organize, and digitally track non-fungible goods.

Homes, cars, and nondigital pets

Imagine a world where home ownership and sales are memorialized on a public blockchain, eliminating the need for title insurance and escrow services.

Also imagine issuing non-fungible tokens in place of car titles. Rather than pay $39.99 for a car history record on CARFAX, as shown in Figure 3-6, you could simply consult the open source blockchain to trace the provenance of a given car. You would be able to see the changes in ownership and a timeline of accidents, service records, and the crossing of state lines — all for free (or a small transaction fee).

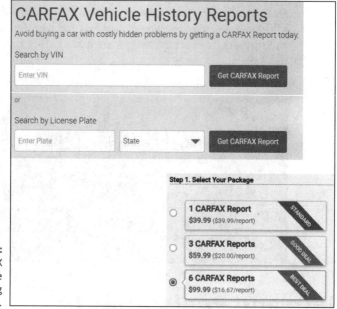

FIGURE 3-6: CARFAX interface and pricing scheme.

And, of course, *CryptoKitties* has provided a solid test case for tracking a nondigital pet's ownership and lineage. In comparison, an American Kennel Club (AKC) certified pedigree, as shown in Figure 3-7, costs $36 and provides only (up to) four generations of ancestry information.

FIGURE 3-7:
An AKC
certificate
of pedigree.

Art, jewelry, wine, and other collectibles

Fine wine, high jewelry, and other masterpieces — expensive items that are rare to experience are rife with fraud. Rudy Kurniawan infamously sold millions of dollars' worth of counterfeit wine, passing off cheaper blends for bottles from prestigious estates such as Domaine de la Romanée-Conti and Château Mouton Rothschild.

REMEMBER

Although NFTs can't detect or solve counterfeit problems, expert inspection coupled with a reliable account of the entire provenance of an item provides assurance — and, if it's of any comfort, only a single counterfeit sale of the original piece is possible.

Imagining the Possibilities

From taxi medallions to concert tickets, any unique and transferrable right is ripe for disintermediated peer-to-peer markets. Introducing the concept of blockchain and native tokens to established ideas and practices has led to hugely valuable and meaningful game changers in *de*centralized *fi*nance, or DeFi (think Uniswap, Chainlink, and Compound), enough to over-shadow the meaningless name changes and fodder for jokes. (Does anyone remember Long Blockchain?)

If you're interested to learn more about these DeFi game chang-ers, check out these websites:

>> **Uniswap (a decentralized exchange):** https://uniswap.org/about

>> **Chainlink (a decentralized oracle):** https://blog.chain.link

>> **Compound (a decentralized lending pool):** https://compound.finance

Overall, the possibilities are vast. What else might be *NFTized* in the future?

2

Buying and Selling NFTs

IN THIS PART . . .

Discover the ins and outs of buying your first NFT.

Uncover the most popular marketplaces to buy and sell NFTs.

Create your own NFT from scratch and for free.

Explore listing your NFT for sale on top NFT marketplaces.

Build your own NFT investment strategy.

Establish a tax plan for your NFT investments.

Chapter **4**

Getting In on the NFT Game

his chapter prepares you to confidently explore the non-fungible token world so that you can buy, create, and sell NFTs on several of the most popular platforms on the Internet. NFTs allow for the creation of new types of digital property that empower their creators. Artists and collectors love NFTs because they have specific properties that make them impossible to fake. NFTs make it possible to create items like digital collectible cards and other types of new digital property.

In this chapter, you discover the ins and outs of the MetaMask hot wallet, how to secure your wallet, and how to navigate and use several of the most popular NFT marketplaces, including OpenSea, Nifty Gateway, and Raribles. You also create and list your first NFT for free and from scratch. Finally, you learn about NFTs as a form of investment and the best ways to capitalize on non-fungible tokens over the next few years.

Knowing the Ins and Outs of Buying NFTs

An *NFT*, or *non-fungible token*, is a digital representation of an asset transferred from one person to another — it typically represents a unique digital item. This emerging technology is already being used by online gaming companies and may soon become the standard for collectibles.

Non-fungible tokens are different from other forms of digital content. They have blockchain-backed certificates that state who owns a photo or a video or another form of online media. Each token is unique and acts as a collector's item, which means that it can't be duplicated — making it rare by design. Non-fungibles have become hugely popular since 2020, with expensive artwork now being sold this way.

Examining the success of early NFTs

Some of the first non-fungibles were the digital collectible cats in the *CryptoKitties* game, which we cover in more detail in Chapter 2. *CryptoKitties* is a blockchain game on the Ethereum network that Canadian studio Dapper Labs developed. It pioneered the ERC-721 token standard, which allows players to purchase, collect, breed, and sell unique virtual cats.

Since its inception, the ERC-721 token standard has expanded and is being used to facilitate the trade of all types of digital media.

The NBA's Top Shot

The mainstream popularity of non-fungible tokens has been linked with the launch of the Top Shot website by the US National Basketball Association (NBA). The site allows users to buy or trade NFTs of their favorite NBA players. NBA fans are an enthusiastic bunch — five months after Top Shot launched, it had over 100,000 buyers and nearly $250 million in sales. The majority of these transactions are made on its peer-to-peer marketplace with a royalty from each sale going to the NBA.

The LeBron James Dunk, one of basketball's most iconic moments, was turned into an NFT and later sold for $200,000. Fans loved purchasing NBA memorabilia to remember the players and games that have been important in their lives. NFTs harnessed this love in a whole new way.

Music artists

NFTs have spread to the music industry as well. Grimes, an artist who has been in the spotlight for several years, sold a series of ten pieces on the Nifty Gateway website for $6 million. The highest-selling piece was the one-of-a-kind music video "Death of the Old," which she auctioned off for $388,938. Grimes also sold several hundred editions of two short music videos titled "Earth" and "Mars" for $7,500 per NFT.

Internet memes

The Nyan Cat Internet meme is just one famous meme that has been turned into an NFT. If you don't remember this particular meme, it's based on a YouTube video from 2011. The animation shows a cat with a Pop-Tart for an abdomen flying through space and leaving behind rainbow trails set to a Japanese pop song. In a 24-hour auction, the creator, Chris Torres, sold his remastered anniversary edition of Nyan Cat for $590,000.

Unusual NFTs

Items that don't necessarily qualify as a form of art have also been turned into non-fungible tokens. For example, you might not think that a tweet is art. However, Jack Dorsey, the founder CEO of Twitter, sold his first tweet as an NFT for $2.9 million. The tweet (published on March 21, 2006) said, "just setting up my twttr." Sina Estavi, a wealthy businessperson who purchased it, compared buying the first tweet to buying the *Mona Lisa* painting. Art and beauty are truly in the eye of the beholder.

Thinking about NFTs as an investment

As with all investments, you need to use your own best judgment in determining the value of the NFT artwork you buy.

We aren't financial advisors, and this is not investment advice.

NFTs can be valued in both subjective and objective ways. In this section, we've put together a few items you need to keep in mind that are linked to a valuable NFT *drop,* a term (borrowed from the music industry) that means "release."

The NFT is a new type of digital asset, and the characteristics of its markets will continue to develop over the years. In a nutshell, always use your best judgment, buy items you innately love, and never invest money you don't have to lose. Happy hunting!

Artist popularity

The artist's popularity before the drop is the biggest determinant of value. If you have heard of the name, it's possible that other people have also and may also want to own a piece of digital art created by that artist.

CryptoPunks undermines this idea a bit because no one would claim that they had any pre-NFT popularity. NFT collectors sell them on marketplaces like OpenSea or Rarible for thousands of dollars in Ether (ETH). The active trade of the *CryptoPunks* creates a price floor and can give you a good idea about how much the market is determining their worth at any given time.

CryptoPunks was also an early NFT project. NFTs can gain value the older they are and the rarer they are. Many of the NFTs from back in 2017, like *CryptoKitties* and *CryptoPunks,* have commanded impressive prices at auction.

Blockchain security

When anyone talks about NFTs, the question of security always comes up. NFTs have gained tracking precisely because they claim to be immutable and fraud proof. They also allow you to own them sovereignly, without relying on a single centralized party to maintain their existence and security. (That's the blockchain part.) Ethereum has emerged as one of the more popular networks for securing NFTs because it's one of the oldest and most secure ways of creating and securing NFTs. When evaluating an NFT's blockchain, you need to consider how decentralized the blockchain is as well as determine whether the blockchain has staying power — in other words, whether it will be able to maintain its popularity into the future.

REMEMBER

Not all NFTs are completely on chain. On chain means that the data that is used to render the digital art is stored on the blockchain. Because data storage can be expensive on a decentralized proof-of-work network, artists will often store the image of the NFT record references on a third-party cloud service like AWS. A few NFTs, like Avastars, Aavegotchis, and Art Blocks drops, are completely hosted on Ethereum.

WARNING

An off chain NFT is a token that represents ownership and does not secure the digital art. If the NFT is on chain, then the underlying art the token represents has the built in redundancy of a distributed data structure.

Understanding the Risks of Hot Wallets like MetaMask

MetaMask is a *hot wallet*, a tool connected to the Internet that enables you to store, receive, and send ETH and other tokens. All web-based wallets are hot wallets and are the most insecure of all the cryptocurrency wallets. By contrast, a *cold wallet* (sometimes referred to as a *hardware wallet* or *offline wallet*) is not connected to the Internet. Given that MetaMask is a hot wallet, it is not a secure way to store value. Only use them for small transactions that you execute right away.

As of this writing, MetaMask has suffered no major hacks. The MetaMask is a *hierarchical deterministic wallet* (HD wallet) that automatically generates a hierarchical tree-like structure of private and public addresses to back up your wallet. You then don't have to manually generate those pairs for backups. MetaMask also has an active community of developers who regularly update its code base. The main risk you face in using MetaMask is from *phishing* attacks, where a scam artist sends you a fraudulent message to trick you into revealing your passwords and usernames.

Phishing attacks are common, and your wallet's password and recovery phrase are the target. Never, under *any* circumstances, give anyone access to your password or passphrase. You can prevent phishing attacks by religiously avoiding opening these items:

>> Pop-up ads

>> Suspicious emails

>> Links in suspicious ads or emails

MetaMask also allows you to manage your identity online. When a dApp wants to run a transaction and write to the Ethereum blockchain, MetaMask acts as a secure interface for you.

That said, the MetaMask wallet's security is insufficient to keep large sums. My rule of thumb is to keep the amount stored here equivalent to what you would be willing to have in your own wallet or purse. If you need to store more tokens, consider using a hardware wallet, like a Trezor or Ledger hardware wallet. Also buy the hardware wallet directly from the manufacturer. In some recent Amazon scams, the devices were compromised before being sent to the buyer.

Comparing hot wallets

MetaMask isn't the only hot wallet out there. We've chosen it to use throughout this book because it has been developed and tested over many years. There are many other wallets you may want to explore, such as Exodus and Jaxx. They are free and work well too.

Weighing the pros and cons of hot wallets

The useful invention MetaMask lets you use the Ethereum blockchain without needing to also operate a full blockchain node. (Running a full blockchain node is a lot of work and occupies a significant portion of your hard drive space.) MetaMask is helpful for beginners who are just getting started with blockchain and NFTs.

This list highlights the pros of MetaMask:

» **Open source:** It's open source software that is constantly being updated. The large development community that contributes to MetaMask keeps improving the software and making it easier and safer to use.

» **Settings:** MetaMask uses hierarchical deterministic settings that allow you to back up your wallet.

» **Integration:** It has integrated with other helpful applications, like ShapeShift and Coinbase, which are cryptocurrency exchange and management platforms. We cover Coinbase in Chapter 2.

And here are the cons:

» **Lack of security:** Like all hot wallets, MetaMask will never be fully secure.

» **Limited access to your info:** MetaMask does have some limited access to your info, which makes some people uncomfortable.

The MetaMask team has come a long way since the product's launch in 2016, and their work has made access to the Ethereum blockchain easy, reliable, and secure.

REMEMBER

The biggest problem with MetaMask is also what makes it so useful: It's a web-based wallet. It will never be as secure as a hardware wallet or a paper wallet.

TECHNICAL STUFF

When you add MetaMask to your browser, you're asked to update your settings by approving a message that says something like this: "Read and change all your data on the websites you visit." Distributed apps (or dApps), like the NFT websites you'll access later in this chapter, access the blockchain. MetaMask needs to inject a web3 JavaScript into each page. This doesn't change the website but allows you to access the website and the blockchain at the same time.

Uncovering Your MetaMask Wallet

MetaMask is a popular cryptowallet that you can install into your choice of many popular browsers. In this section, we show you how to set up your new wallet, protect it from theft, and add funds to it.

The creators of MetaMask wanted to make a wallet that was both easy to use and secure. In addition, they wanted their wallet to allow new users to interact with Web 3.0 websites, like OpenSea. (We talk about OpenSea in greater detail later in this chapter.) You can think of *Web 3.0* as the ongoing effort to make the Internet more intelligent and connected, and MetaMask is your interface to this new web.

MetaMask handles account management and connects the user to the Ethereum blockchain. MetaMask, which is a wallet for Ether as well as ERC20 tokens, allows you to manage your Ethereum private keys via your web browser. It also allows users to log on to websites that have MetaMask integration. This is pretty cool because it enables you to run Ethereum dApps in your favorite browser without running a full Ethereum node. Before MetaMask, you would need to download and sync the full blockchain on your device, a task that was considerably more difficult for the average person to manage.

Installing MetaMask

Getting up and running with MetaMask is *easy.* In this section, we show you the instructions for installing MetaMask via these three popular browsers: Chrome, Firefox, and (Tiana's personal favorite) Brave.

TIP

If you don't use one of these browsers but would like to, we suggest downloading Brave from its official site, at https://brave.com.

MetaMask for Chrome

To download MetaMask for Chrome, open Chrome and follow these steps:

1. **Navigate to** https://metamask.io.

2. **Click the Download Now Button.**

You're sent to the Chrome Store.

3. **From the MetaMask page at the Chrome Store, click Add to Chrome.**

4. **From the pop-up menu that appears, choose Add Extension.**

That's about it. A small Chrome icon appears in the upper-right corner of your browser. All you need to do to open MetaMask is click the icon. Skip to the later section "Securing your MetaMask wallet for Chrome and Firefox" to see how to secure your wallet.

MetaMask for Firefox

To download MetaMask for Firefox, open Firefox and follow these steps:

1. **Navigate to** https://metamask.io.

2. **Click the Download Now Button.**

This step sends you to the Firefox Add-Ons page.

3. **Click the Add to Firefox Button.**

4. **From the pop-up that appears, click Add.**

You now have a brand-new MetaMask wallet. A small fox icon is added to the upper-right corner of your browser — just click the icon to open MetaMask. Skip to the "Securing your MetaMask wallet for Chrome and Firefox" section, later in this chapter, to see how to secure your wallet.

MetaMask for Brave

The Brave browser has MetaMask already built into it, so it's *easy* to access as you only need to turn it on. Open Brave and follow these steps:

1. **Navigate to** https://metamask.io.

2. **Click the Download now button.**

3. **Click the Install MetaMask for Brave button.**

You're directed to the Brave app store website.

4. **Click the Add to Brave button.**

5. **Click the Add Extension.**

6. **Click the Get Started button.**

7. **Click the Create a Wallet button.**

8. **Click the No Thanks button.**

You could also click the I Agree button to share your data with the Metamask development team.

9. **When prompted, create a unique password and write it down someplace safe.**

Do not skip this step.

You're given a master passphrase consisting of 12 words.

WARNING

The blockchain has no customer service department — *you* are responsible for your own account recovery. The 12 words you're given in a master passphrase allow you to recover your account.

MetaMask prompts you to put the 12 words into the same order they were given to you on the next page. Before this step, you have a few options to secure your password and your passphrase: You can write it down in a secure place that is not online or on your computer. Writing it down on multiple pieces of paper and storing each one in two or three secure locations such as a vault or a lockable file cabinet is a good option. If you can laminate your password and your backup phrase, do that now, too.

10. **Enter the words as directed and click All Done.**

Securing your MetaMask wallet for Chrome and Firefox

If you've installed MetaMask for Chrome or Firefox, follow these steps to secure your wallet:

1. **From your open Chrome or Firefox browser, click the fox icon in the upper-right corner.**

2. **In the middle of the new page that appears, click the Get Started button.**

3. **Click the Create a Wallet button.**

4. **On the Help Us Improve MetaMask page, click I Agree.**

5. **When prompted, create a unique password and write it down someplace safe.**

   Do not skip this step.

   After creating your own password, you're given a master passphrase consisting of 12 words.

WARNING

   These 12 words allow you to recover your account. The blockchain does not have a customer service department. You are responsible for your own account recovery.

   MetaMask prompts you to put the 12 words into the same order they were given to you on the next page. Before this step, you have a few options to secure your password and your passphrase. Do not use a password manager. It is better to hand write your passphrase on multiple pieces of paper and storing each in two or three locations. A vault or a lockable file cabinet are good options. If you can laminate your password and your backup phrase, do so now too.

6. **Enter the words as directed and click All Done.**

Buying Ether for Your MetaMask Wallet

If you don't already own ETH (Ethereum's native cryptocurrency), you can buy small amounts from within your MetaMask wallet application. Larger amounts are allowed if you go through the customer identification requirements with Wyre, the Ethereum payment vendor.

REMEMBER

The *Wyre* payment process allows you a straightforward way to purchase cryptocurrency with Apple Pay or your credit card. Don't forget to hold only small amounts of cryptocurrencies in hot wallets like MetaMask.

To get your hands on some ETH, follow these steps:

1. **In the browser where you previously installed MetaMask, open your MetaMask wallet by clicking the Fox icon in the upper-right corner.**

2. **Sign in to your wallet using your username and password and then click the Buy button.**

3. **Click the Continue to Wyre button.**

   A new window opens and loads the Wyre payment page: https://pay.sendwyre.com/purchase.

4. **Select how much you want to buy and your payment method (Apple Pay or credit card).**

If the Wyre app doesn't work for you, you can also buy ETH through a Coinbase account, which you can set up at www.coinbase.com. If you need more support in setting up Coinbase, see Chapter 2; for help with facilitating a wallet-to-wallet transfer, see Tiana Laurence's book *Blockchain For Dummies* (Wiley Publishing).

The new tokens will appear in your MetaMask wallet shortly after you purchase them or transfer them from another. The time you have to wait will depend on the network speed. Once they arrive, you're ready to buy your first NFT.

Exploring NFT Marketplaces

You can easily get lost in all the different variations and platforms that allow you to buy, sell, and create NFTs. In this section, we introduce three platforms that enable you to buy, sell, and even create NFTs.

Navigating the OpenSea of NFTs

The large, peer-to-peer marketplace for user-owned digital goods, OpenSea, offers collectibles, domain names, digital art, gaming items, and other assets — all backed by blockchains. OpenSea lets you buy, sell, create, transfer, and browse NFTs in one easy-to-use marketplace, and it's blessed with a large community of passionate users, developers, and creators.

Devin Finzer created OpenSea in 2017 with his co-founder, Alex Atallah. Finzer had recently sold his previous company, Claim-dog, to Credit Karma. His experience with working at large tech giants like Google and studying computer science and mathematics at Brown University helped him see the potential of new emerging digital economies enabled by blockchain technology.

The OpenSea marketplace was quickly adopted by the creators of all the new digital items built with blockchains and evolved rapidly into a billion-dollar marketplace. The tools that were built allow developers to create rich, integrated digital assets and sell them.

Common token types on OpenSea

Several important token types are available on OpenSea. These include token standards, such as ERC20, ERC1155, and ERC721. These different standards allow users to program their assets in distinct ways that are worth knowing:

» **ERC20 is a fungible token that's created with a smart contract.** An ERC20 token contract keeps track of fungible tokens. *Fungible* in this context means that any single token is precisely equal to any other token. The ERC20 tokens have no special rights or behaviors associated with them. ERC20 tokens are useful for tasks such as creating a cryptocurrency and securing voting rights.

» **The ERC1155 is a token standard used to create fungible and non-fungible (unique) assets, such as digital cards, pets, and in-game skins.** A more complex standard than ERC20, it allows developers to use a single smart contract to represent multiple tokens at once.

>> **ERC721 represents ownership of tokens — ERC721 tokens are used to track items, each of which has unique attributes.** ERC721 is an older standard for non-fungible digital assets. Though similar to ERC1155, ERC721 does differ in that it has no concept of a balance. Each token created as an ERC721 is unique and non-fungible, and it either exists or it doesn't.

TECHNICAL STUFF

Developers created the ERC1155 to help them manage the fees tokens incurred on their blockchain. This token standard leads to massive gas savings for projects that require multiple tokens. Rather than deploy a new contract for each token type using an ERC721, a single ERC1155 token contract can represent multiple tokens, reducing deployment costs and complexity.

Buying NFTs on OpenSea

Buying an NFT is pretty easy on OpenSea, especially if you already own some bitcoin or ETH and have a MetaMask wallet set up. In the browser where you installed MetaMask, go to the OpenSea website (`https://opensea.io`), click the fox icon, and log in to your MetaMask wallet.

You can browse OpenSea categories by clicking Marketplace. Each category shows trending collections, recently listed items, and newly minted items. To find and buy NFTs on OpenSea, follow these steps:

1. **Under Marketplace in the top navigation, select Art.**

This step takes you to the Explore Art page, which lists the latest NFT art. You can use the search bar to look for artists you enjoy or browse what's available.

For this exercise, we're searching for one of our favorite NFT creators: Artificial Intelligence Art V2. It creates unique pieces of art based on classical paintings. The AI model was trained by analyzing millions of images from famous artists such as Pablo Picasso, Mark Rothko, and Claude Monet. It produces a limited collection of interesting artworks that are unique yet familiar.

2. **Type The Aftermath of Uncertainty 1583 in the search bar.**

3. **Click the image of *The Aftermath of Uncertainty* to go to its page, where you see its details, including trading history.**

   The trading history (scroll down to see it) shows who has owned the NFT and the price that was paid. Every NFT has an owner, a creator, and a history, and this information is verifiable. Each item's page also has a Details section, where you can verify details about the contract used to create it and other important information, such as which blockchain secures the NFT and whether the image is stored in one central location or across multiple location.

4. **If you locate a piece of art you want to buy, click the Buy Now button.**

   Your MetaMask wallet pulls up a transaction page that allows you to add the NFT to your wallet.

   After you buy the NFT, it is associated with the MetaMask wallet that you used to buy it.

REMEMBER

Make sure that your wallet is secure. If you're unsure, refer to the "Installing MetaMask" section, earlier in this chapter.

Creating your own NFT on OpenSea

Setting up your first collection on OpenSea is simple. This section covers creating an OpenSea collection and adding your very own NFTs to it.

You can use any sketching software to create a digital piece of art, so use whichever digital art creation tool you like. In this example, we're uploading an abstract piece of art Tiana created with the free sketching software on https://sketch.io.

OpenSea accepts a variety of file formats for images, videos, audio, and 3D models. Though the site suggests keeping the file size at smaller than 20MB, it nevertheless can support file sizes up to 40MB, at the time of writing. These file types are supported by OpenSea: GIF, GLB, GLTF JPG, MP3, MP4, OGG, PNG, SVG, WAV, and WEBM. (If you go for the upper limit of 40MB, you may encounter some speed issues.)

The sketch.io website has some older icons at the time of writing, but Figure 4-1 shows the download page with these options selected:

» **Format:** JPEG, one of OpenSea's acceptable file types

» **DPI:** 300 — the higher the resolution, the higher the quality of the image

» **Size To:** Scale

» **Size:** 2.0x

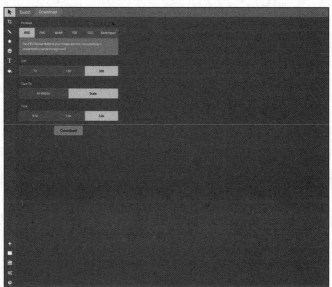

FIGURE 4-1:
The sketch.io download page.

When you download your artwork, be sure to name it something creative and save it to a folder you can easily navigate to later. Nice job! You now have an original piece of art that you can turn into an NFT. (Figure 4-2 shows a Tiana Laurence abstract original created on sketch.io for this chapter.)

FIGURE 4-2:
A Tiana
Laurence
original,
created on
sketch.io.

With your artwork completed, it's now time to set up your first collection on OpenSea. Here's how:

1. Go to opensea.io.

2. Click the Profile icon and choose My Collections.

With your MetaMask wallet installed on your browser, it should log you into OpenSea automatically. Otherwise follow Step 3.

3. If prompted, log in with your wallet.

Your wallet will be your identity on OpenSea.

If you haven't yet set up a wallet, see the "Installing MetaMask" section, earlier in this chapter.

4. Click the Create a Collection link at the top of the My Collections page.

5. Enter a name for your collection as well as a description.

You now have a space on the OpenSea marketplace! To add a piece of art to your collection for others to view, just follow these steps:

1. From your collection page, click Add Item at the top of the page.

You're sent to a new page, prompting you to upload your artwork.

Under Create New Item is a box you can use to drag and drop your image, video, audio, or 3D model file.

2. **Drag the image file to the indicated box at the top of the page.**

3. **Using the page's text boxes, add a short description and other details.**

4. **Scroll to the bottom of the page and click the Create button.**

Congratulations! You have created your first NFT. You can now share it on social media. (If you had a great time doing this, tag me in a tweet at @LaurenceTiana with your new NFT.)

The Nifty Gateway

Nifty Gateway is a premium digital art auction platform for non-fungible tokens. The famous Winklevoss twins purchased it from founders Griffin and Duncan Cock Foster — another set of twins. Nifty Gateway has sold NFTs created by popular artists such as Beeple, Grimes, Billelis, and other internationally regarded artists. Nifty Gateway, which has a partnership with the auction house Sotheby's, has positioned itself as a premium platform for NFT collectors.

Discovering Nifties and drops

Nifty Gateway calls its rare digital items *Nifties*, but don't let that confuse you — *Nifty* is just another (hipper) name for NFTs. Nifties follow the same popular ERC-721 standard as other tokens. Each Nifty is its own one-of-a-kind digital item. And, like other platforms, Nifty Gateway is a helpful place to find cryptocollectibles and crypto art.

Nifty Gateway offers an easy way to buy NFTs with your credit card or debit card. Most other platforms at the time of this writing require you to use a cryptocurrency like ETH. The platform also allows you to buy NFTs from popular cryptogames and applications, such as *CryptoKitties*, OpenSea, and *Gods Unchained*.

An interesting feature of Nifty Gateway involves *drops*, a specific time when an artist releases a limited number of new digital art pieces. This is how the artist Grimes released her NFT *WarNymph*, with her collaborator, Mac Boucher. Within a few minutes, they sold all their artwork.

TIP

Drops have become popular with collectors because they allow you to not only see new work from amazing artists but also capitalize on your purchase by reselling them on an NFT marketplace. This strategy works a lot like buying popular concert tickets and then reselling them on ticket reseller websites, like StubHub. The difference is that Nifties drops are sold directly by the artists. You can buy these NFTs during a set time or purchase them from their original owners on secondary marketplaces.

Setting up a Nifty account and making a purchase

To set up your Nifty account, follow these steps:

1. **Navigate to** https://niftygateway.com.

2. **Click the Sign Up / Sign In button.**

3. **On the sign up page fill in account information to create a new account for yourself.**

   Nifty Gateway sends you a confirmation email with a code.

4. **Check your email and copy-and-paste into the validation box the code you receive.**

When it comes to researching and buying an NFT, it's easy. Just do the following:

1. **Navigate back to the Nifty Gateway home page:** https://niftygateway.com.

2. **Click the Drops button in the upper-right corner.**

   This step directs you to a new drops page, listing all the upcoming events (with dates).

3. **Click the artist who's featured for the day.**

This step directs you to a page with information describing the NFT that's up for sale.

The first section shows information about the artist and the collection that the artist has publicized.

The NFTs that are available for sale appear under the Explore Open Collection heading.

4. **Click on one of the NFTs to bring up another page with more information about how many editions have been allowed for that piece of art.**

When you find an NFT you love, you can bid on it by clicking the Bid button that is in the description below the image of the NFT. From within the Nifty Gateway website, you buy NFTs with your credit card, just like normal online shopping websites.

REMEMBER

NFTs are artwork first, so they might not be a productive investment. Their popularity (and therefore their value) may decrease over time. Don't spend more money on NFTs than you have to lose, and buy only what you truly like.

Rarible's decentralized governance

Rarible, a decentralized marketplace for non-fungible tokens, was founded in 2017 by Alexei Falin and Alexander Salnikov, both from Russia. Rarible launched to the public three years later, in 2020. As on other NFT platforms, you can create and sell your tokenized art. Unlike on other platforms, it provides a diverse suite of services that are quite artist-friendly. Rarible enables hi-resolution files and hidden messages. You can also set up smart contracts, which allow you to collect royalties on your artwork. For example, you can receive a fee whenever your artwork changes hands. Rarible is a great way of generating income for artists. However, this can be circumvented if the NFT is resold on a platform that doesn't support the same royalty system.

Rarible's NFT marketplace differences go even deeper. From the beginning, it has been driven by community engagement through a new type of company, called a *decentralized autonomous organization (DAO)*. Unlike centralized services, a *DAO* is a non-custodial NFT minting platform and marketplace. Noncustodial means that there is not a central party in charge. Rarible's DAO has created a strong community of artists and NFT lovers that manage the platform collectively.

As a community member, you can decide on the platform's future using its native governance token, RARI. (A *governance token*, for all you cryptocurrency newbies out there, is a type of cryptocurrency that grants voting power on a blockchain.) RARI enables the most active creators and collectors on Rarible to vote on platform upgrades and participate in curation and moderation.

REMEMBER

To be clear, you can't purchase RARI, and it has no market value — you earn it by actively participating on the platform. Creators, sellers, and buyers on the Rarible marketplace receive RARI through weekly distributions according to their weekly activity level, like purchases and sales volumes.

Creating an NFT on Rarible takes only a few minutes. The platform has a simple interface that allows you to publish an NFT and set up smart contracts with royalty percentages and auctions for your art.

The Rarible platform works to solve intellectual property payment problems, fraud, and licensing paperwork issues by offering artists the ability to tokenize their works of art and guarantee their origin and ownership.

WARNING

Rarible isn't perfect — it has some issues it needs to overcome. For example, creators can game Rarible's DOA system by *washing* their NFTs, this is a scam where a user buys their own artwork to gain RARI tokens. Keep in mind as well that Rarible at the time of this writing isn't yet a complete DAO. This means your vote is more of a suggestion to the Rarible team. The company still decides what to work on — which is probably for the best, given that the project is still quite new.

Getting up and running on Rarible

You set up an account with Rarible by connecting your wallet to the site. To do so, go to https://rarible.com and click Connect Wallet in the upper-right corner of the screen. Select MetaMask or the name of whichever wallet service you're using.

When you're signed into your wallet, you're also logged in to Rarible. You can then adjust your admin settings by following these steps:

1. **Click the My Items button at the top of the page or navigate to** https://rarible.com/settings.

2. **From this page, update your display name and connect your social media accounts, if you want.**

3. **Click the Update Profile button to save your changes.**

    If this step creates a new pop-up from your MetaMask wallet, go ahead and click through the prompts. This can happen when the website is confirming your identity. If you have a pending transaction in your wallet for example, it will prevent you from updating your user information on Rarible. You will need to clear the transaction from your wallet by adding funds or canceling the transaction. After you clear your wallet of pending transaction, it can then authenticate you for Rarible.

Creating an auction with a royalty structure

Before diving into the steps needed to conduct a Rarible auction, you first need to create a piece of digital artwork, using Sketchpad or another sketching software.

With your artwork in hand, follow these steps:

1. **Navigate to the Rarible website at** https://rarible.com/.

2. **Click Sign in with Metamask.**

    If you have not yet set up your Metamask wallet, go back to earlier in the chapter and follow the instructions to set up your wallet.

3. Click the Create button at the top of the page.

4. Under the Create Collectible section, click Multiple.

5. Click the Choose a File button.

This button will open a new window that will allow you to search for the file for your art on your computer.

6. Search for the name of your art file using the search bar.

Your file will appear in the window as you type in its name.

7. Select the art file by clicking on it from within the window.

8. Click the Open button on the bottom right corner of the window.

Your art will appear on the Rarible page and you will continue the rest of the instructions from within your browser.

9. Click the Open for bids button.

This step allows that market to bid for your new NFT.

10. Under the Choose Collection section, click Rari.

11. Add the title, a description, and the royalties percentage you want each time your piece trades hands.

12. Add the number of copies you want to make.

13. Click the Create Item button.

14. Navigate to your MetaMask wallet and click Approve.

If you haven't yet added funds to your MetaMask wallet, you can find instructions earlier in this chapter. There will be a gas fee for securing your NFT on the Ethereum blockchain. The fee price is not fixed and will be dynamic. (For more on gas fees, see Chapter 6.)

15. Navigate back to the Rarible website and click Start.

You may need to refresh the page to see your NFT.

Congratulations! You've successfully created your own NFT auction for multiple copies of the same piece and set a royalty structure so that you get paid every time your NFT is traded.

Chapter **5**

Investing In NFTs

This chapter covers the new world of NFT investing. Here you can explore investment strategies, including looking at what types of NFTs you can invest in. You're also introduced to the rules and regulatory bodies that govern all types of investment, including NFTs.

Whether you're considering serious investing, enjoying collecting, or wanting to be on the leading edge of investing (or if you're simply curious), NFTs have a lot to offer. Sometimes the only way to truly understand such a new market is to explore it. Exploring marketplaces introduces you to the wide variety of available tokens. You can also get a feel for the pricing and how different marketplaces curate, list, and sell their assets.

REMEMBER

As with any investment, you should do as much research as possible and never invest more than you can afford to lose. We also advise you to keep up with the changing market, as changes in supply, demand, technology, and regulation will likely keep the market in flux for some time.

We are not financial experts, and the information in this chapter is not meant to serve as investment or tax advice. This chapter does not take the place of guidance from professional investment advisors and accountants.

Understanding NFTs Are Not Cryptocurrency

On a technical level, NFTs are similar to cryptocurrency in that they exist as a digital record on the blockchain. The difference between NFTs and cryptocurrency is that each NFT is unique. If you own a single bitcoin, for example, you can trade that bitcoin for another bitcoin and it will have the same market value. This is often described as *fungibility* — an asset's ability to be exchanged with another individual asset of the same type and implies equal value between the assets.

On the blockchain, any bitcoin is the same as any other. The same goes for Ether on the Ethereum blockchain, Litecoin, and even Dogecoin on their respective networks. Millions of dollars are exchanged globally for these types of assets, and they attract lots of buyers.

NFTs are different. Each non-fungible token has a unique value and, though they can be traded, they cannot simply be swapped out for another. Although the cryptocurrency market is quite volatile, at any given moment one bitcoin holds the same value as any other. Each NFT has its own value and can change at any moment with no relationship to the value of other NFTs.

The NFT has value if it has a willing-and-able buyer and seller. It may have a market of one, or no one may want to buy it at any price. There is speculation that the market for NFTs may crash, just like the TY Beanie Babies of the 1990s.

Introducing NFT Investing

The investment world has been changing quickly with the invention of cryptocurrencies and new types of digital assets, like *equity tokens* (security tokens that work like traditional stock assets) and NFTs. Regulation within the space hasn't fully caught up with the global enthusiasm for these new types of assets.

Traditional investing has been limited for the general population. You typically would work with an investment broker or financial advisor — individuals who help you navigate the complex world of stocks, bonds, and investment funds. These types of investments have slow and more reliable returns, and the investment professionals who help you are regulated by government bodies.

This wasn't always the case. The 1920s saw wild speculation and fraud that left millions of people in a perilous economic state. The Securities and Exchange Commission (SEC), established in 1934 as an independent US federal regulatory agency, serves to protect investors and to enforce federal securities laws. It was part of the New Deal the U.S. created to fight the economic consequences of the Great Depression and prevent any future financial disasters brought on by fraud or hubris.

To further protect the public, the U.S. Congress passed the Securities Act of 1933, which required the registration of most securities sales in the United States or securities that are made available to American citizens. This act helps prevent securities fraud by requiring that investors receive truthful financial data about public securities. It also gave the Federal Trade Commission (FTC) the power to stop securities sales and put people in jail.

REMEMBER

New *financial instruments* — those real or virtual documents created by way of blockchain technology that represent a legal agreement involving monetary value — are subject to the FTC and SEC. Keep this statement in mind as you explore NFTs, because they may be a financial instrument and subject to regulation and laws based on your citizenship, country, and — if you choose to sell them — the buyer's citizenship and country.

The SEC evaluates digital assets like NFTs similarly to traditional assets to determine whether they are securities. At the
time we wrote this chapter, NFTs had not been the subject of
interpretative guidance by the SEC nor had enforcement action
been taken against the creators of NFTs. However, NFTs can be
used to defraud investors or for money laundering, and the
United States or other governments are likely to step in and regulate the space. Sometimes that takes years, and it may take
even longer for enforcements to occur.

A simple way to think about this is if you buy an NFT related to
an existing asset, sold as a collectible with a public record of
authenticity on a blockchain, it probably isn't a financial security. Your purchase would be just like buying a painting or
another piece of art. However, NFTs can have many types of
properties that might easily make them a financial instrument.
If you purchase an NFT that promises you a return on your
investment, it might be a security — a real estate investment
sold as an NFT that promises a dividend, for example, or a roy-
ally stream from digital art may also be a security as it would
likely not pass the Howey Test. (The Howey Test determines
what qualifies as an "investment contract" in the U.S. and what
type of assets are subject to U.S. securities laws.) When you are
examining an investment opportunity and are not sure if it's an
investment contract, you can look for these four criteria:

>> It involves an investment of money.

>> It is a common enterprise.

>> Profit is expected.

>> Such profit is derived from the efforts of others.

Deciding Whether NFT Investing Is for You

Before developing an NFT investment strategy, first ask yourself
whether this type of investment is right for you. You can choose
many other investment opportunities that have more history,

predictability, and available market research. As with all highly volatile and speculative investments, do *not* bet the farm on NFTs.

WARNING

Invest only amounts you can afford to never see again. This strategy helps keep you safe financially and saves you from undue stress.

When and if you see greater demand and a higher price for the assets you own, it's fun and exciting. And if no one ever thinks what you own is interesting or valuable, it isn't a loss to you, because you stayed within your means and, hopefully, loved what you bought.

Here are two reasons that people generally invest in NFTs:

>> **Getting in on the ground floor of new assets:** Owning one of the first NFTs of its kind definitely carries a certain prestige.

>> **Earning money:** Right now, some people are making a fortune buying and selling NFTs. Unfortunately, little data is available for the secondary markets. Still, you'll find plenty of stories of people striking it rich.

NFTs seem to be enjoying a moment similar to the early days of cryptocurrency. Some people made so much money by purchasing Bitcoin and other tokens early on that everyone wanted to get into the game. Some did well, but others invested in new coins that failed to gain or even retain their value. They lost significant capital in the market fluctuations.

NFT Investing Strategies for Beginners

NFTs have investors excited by the significant untapped global opportunities available. NFTs may also be a bubble about to burst, much like the TY Beanie Baby crazy of the 1990s. The truth is likely somewhere in the middle.

Some NFTs might offer golden opportunities for investment, and others may quickly become valueless. In some ways, investing in NFTs is like any other sort of investing and undoubtedly comes with risk. Being well informed is your best approach.

You might decide to collect NFTs for fun. Many people collect coins or stamps for the joy of collecting. Yes, sometimes collections are extremely valuable, but many collectors feel just fine never selling what they've collected. If you, on the other hand, want to take a shot and build value or wealth with NFTs, you need to do some homework.

Jumping into NFTs without enough knowledge would be like investing in traditional art with no understanding of art or the value of art. You could be stuck with an item that has no financial value. If you extend yourself too far on such investments, it can lead to financial ruin.

Valuing your NFT

In many ways, an NFT is just a digital version of a traditional collectible item or digital modern art item. Baseball cards, coins, art, documents, and even cars can be collectibles. What gives them value is their scarcity and desirability. The more something is desired and the lower its supply, the higher its value. You still need to have willing and able buyers or else no market exists, no matter how rare the item.

NFTs are similar to all these items but at the same time different. The NFT itself is just a record that has been recorded on a blockchain that verifies ownership and provenance; an NFT often doesn't also contain the underlying digital content. Blockchains have limited capacity, and digital media files are quite large and expensive to store in this manner on most traditional blockchains.

The technology behind NFTs does help create some of that value. Because scarcity is related to the value of collectibles, digital creations became challenging to collect. Digital works can often be copied with no loss of quality — which can make it difficult to "own" a digital asset. NFTs fix that problem by allowing artists to create limited editions or even create a token for the original and selling the rights to a collector. These items can represent the value of the asset; in other words, they represent what someone is willing to pay for that asset.

You can choose from several methods to determine the value of an NFT. The consensus around the value of any asset can be based on brand, scarcity, or market. If you're familiar with other collectibles, you may find these factors familiar.

Brand

Brand, in this context, is basically a question of who created or is related to the NFT asset. One of the most expensive collectibles sold on NBA Top Shot (https://nbatopshot.com) is a video clip of LeBron James, which we discuss further in the later section "Discovering the Best-Performing NFTs." LeBron's brand has value — though collectors may be impressed by the exact move demonstrated in the clip, the most significant value is the person. The NFT world right now has drawn some big names, Coors, Coco Cola, the NBA, and artists like Beeple and Grimes. Though finding a valuable NFT not related to a known artist's brand is possible, it's much more difficult to establish long-term value.

Scarcity

Scarcity is one of the most critical factors in determining NFT value. If an artist releases a single copy of a work, it has more value than releasing 10,000. Fortunately, because scarcity is such an important factor, most marketplaces make it clear how many of each piece are available. Thus, creators and marketplaces can quickly impact value through scarcity by controlling the number of copies released.

Market

The final piece of determining the value of an NFT is the markets, or NFT marketplaces, where they're sold. Investors can look at the markets to determine the price of earlier sales, sales of similar items, and, in some cases, appraisals.

Choosing your strategy

If you have decided you're ready to enter the unstable world of NFTs, the first step involves research. Searching for NFT investment opportunities will show you that the current state of the industry resembles the wild west. Hundreds of thousands of NFTs are available from dozens of NFT marketplaces. (We explore ten of those marketplaces in Chapter 12.)

WARNING

Be *sure*, before making a purchase, that you're dealing with a legitimate marketplace and that the underlying asset is authentic — anyone can create an NFT and call it an original. Because of the decentralized nature of NFTs and the blockchain behind them, no official source vets the quality and reputation of these marketplaces.

Start with a small investment within a genre of NFTs that you love, because making investments that you understand and enjoy researching is a good route. After you purchase an asset, you spend a lot of time reading about it and watching the market.

As you gain knowledge and confidence, you will likely start to invest more. As an investor, Tiana sets investment goals, which enable her to make calculated decisions even when a market is hot. Having an investment plan — and sticking to it — can help you make reasoned decisions, no matter the asset class.

A key metric Tiana looks for is *trading volume*, the number of buyers and sellers that are active at any one time. This is a bit tricky with NFTs because they are in a *thin market*, which has few buyers and sellers.

WARNING

A trick used by scam artists involves selling an asset repeatedly between accounts they own to inflate the value and create false volume signals. In the cases of NFTs, you need to research using unconventional sources like Reddit and Twitter. Anyone can post there, however, so be wary of *pump and dumpers* who are trying to inflate the value of an asset. This problem is, unfortunately, extremely common in the crypto space.

As an investor, Tiana picks an arbitrarily conservative *target return*, which refers to the future value, or profit, you can expect to see on your investment, such as 10 percent. You need to do your own research and pick a target return number you'd be happy with, because it can help you know when to sell. The legendary investor Warren Buffett advises investors to buy when everyone else is selling and to sell when everyone else is buying. Tiana uses this method.

Another practice Tiana uses is to sell below what she perceives is the top of the market. Again, she picks an arbitrary number like 10 percent below what she believes the top of the market will be, which helps her to exit an asset instead of riding a crash down. Trading at the height of a market is extremally difficult to judge.

Discovering the Best-Performing NFTs

Buyers value NFTs for many different reasons. For some investors, NFTs are a form of art. For others, buying an NFT may signal to their social group their power and inclusion. *Social signaling* is the idea that you're part of a group and have a high status by way of ownership of a particular object.

To understand NFTs and clarify the benefits and risks of investing, review some of the best-performing NFTs.

Here's a list of several unique NFTs and some of the factors that drove their price:

>> **LeBron James, "Cosmic" dunk video (created in 2019; sold for $208,000):** This NFT is part of the NBA Top Shot NFT exchange. For some, Top Shot brings back memories of collecting trading cards — and it works in a similar way. Collectors buy packs and sometimes find that one *card* (an individual clip documenting moments from NBA games) in the collection that's especially valuable. "Cosmic" came from a pack of 49 cards. The collections range in price,

starting at $9 for common cards to close to $1,000 for packs likely to contain rare cards.

» *Rick and Morty,* **"The Best I Could Do" artwork (created in 2021; sold for $1 million):** A staple of Cartoon Network's *Adult Swim, Rick and Morty* was created by Justin Roland. Roland sold off a collection of 18 original art pieces from the show for a million dollars. It was the biggest sale to date on the NFT auction house Nifty Gateway. Rick and Morty enjoy a large fan base and have a cult-like following.

» **CryptoPunk #7523 (a pixel-art character created in 2017; sold for $11.8 million):** It's part of 10,000 pixel-art characters made by Larva Labs, which started initially as a small, internal project at Google. *CryptoPunks* are a fixture in the NFT world, and ownership has created social signaling. See Chapter 13 for more about CryptoPunk #7523 and other *CryptoPunks.*

» **Axie Infinity's virtual game Genesis Estate (created in 2021; sold for $1.5 million):** It's virtual land inside the cryptogame Axie. As with real land, its value boiled down to location. The estate, which is in a prime location, offers a unique aesthetic.

» **The first tweet from Twitter CEO Jack Dorsey (originally created in 2006; turned into an NFT and sold for $2.9 million in 2021):** Twitter has become incredibly important, culturally and historically. Although the tweet itself was originally created way before the creation of the first blockchain, the NFT was created to represent the first tweet ever, which definitely has collector appeal.

» **The 2021 Doge meme (turned into an NFT; sold for a whopping $4.4 million):** Memes are cultural touchpoints that show up in many forms, and ownership of a meme is the ultimate social signal. The Doge meme, starring an adorable Shiba Inu, was extremely popular within the crypto space because it conveys the inside joke that anyone can make a cryptocurrency.

>> **Beeple: *EVERYDAYS — FIRST 5000 DAYS* (digital artwork created in 2021; sold for $69.3 million):** This piece of purely digital artwork (it's more akin to fine modern art), which was the first one sold by a major auction house (Christie's), is made up of 5,000 images taken over 13 years. It was sold to Singapore-based NFT collectors MetaKovan and Twobadour. See Chapter 13 for more about this piece, and other pieces, of Beeple's art.

Exploring Popular NFT Types

Many types of NFTs exist, and new token standards are being developed all the time. In this section, we show you several of the most popular types of NFTs.

Digital art

Digital art is a broad category for NFTs, which has enjoyed some of the highest selling prices. It's also the oldest type of NFT. Kevin McCoy's *Quantum* was the first NFT ever minted. Creating and selling within this category is extremely easy, and many platforms exist that allow *anyone* to create NFT digital art.

Collectibles

Collectibles are also a large category within the NFT market. These types of NFTs are a lot like traditional baseball cards and stamps. NBA Top Shot, the largest sports collectibles platform, has enabled millions of dollars of sales and empowered a new generation of enthusiasts.

Games

Games have also benefited from blockchain. In-game assets are a perfect match for NFTs, having the highest sales volume of any segment: In 2020, more than 600,000 in-game assets were sold. This number included digital land, skins, and characters.

NFTs, which allow players to have more power and control over their digital assets in-game, are disruptive to the normal game economics that favor the game makers over the players.

Music

Music sold as an NFT has also become popular. It allows artists to sell music directly to their fans, and for their fans to have extra perks that were traditionally hard to facilitate. The music industry is still adjusting to the massive shift toward streaming. Artists are no longer at the mercy of record companies to record and promote physical album sales, and independent artists are finding new ways to monetize and share their content. Musicians can now tokenize their music and sell it directly to fans. In many cases, fans can receive exclusive content and artwork that can't be found anywhere else.

NFTs in the music segment can lead to some significant transactions. In February of 2021, the DJ and producer 3LAU sold $12 million of NFTs. The offerings included a custom song, access to never-before-heard music, custom artwork, and new versions of existing songs.

Popular memes

It's one of the strangest categories: memes that have been turned into NFTs. Older popular memes such as Disaster Girl, Nylon Cat, and Overly Attached Girlfriend have sold for hundreds of thousands of dollars. Memes have characteristics like universality — they belong to a cultural moment in time and to the people that participated within the subculture that spawned its creation and popularization. Ownership of a meme seems to be in opposition to the idea of scarcity, so this is a unique space.

Reporting NFT Gains and Paying Taxes on NFTs

If you delve into the world of NFT investing, you want to be prepared for the tax implications. If you thought that the decentralized, digital nature of NFTs would let you off the hook with the IRS, think again. There are two types of NFT revenue:

>> The income that NFT creators earn when they sell an NFT

>> The money investors earn by selling NFTs

Most investors don't need to worry about how creators are taxed but, just for information, it's simple: NFT creators treat income from selling as ordinary income. In the case of freelance creators, it's self-employment income subject to self-employment tax.

For U.S. investors, NFTs are treated as any other collectible under Internal Revenue Code Section 408(m)(2), which means that gains made from selling NFTs are subject to capital gains taxes. High-income earners can expect to pay a higher tax rate on NFT gains.

As expected, the IRS is still catching up with the brand-new NFT phenomenon. No reporting mechanism exists yet, so both buyers and sellers need to keep their own detailed records for tax purposes. How you report gains from NFTs to the IRS again depends on your relationship to the assets. Creators simply report them in their business profit-and-loss (P&L) form. They can deduct any fees or expenses related to the creation of the NFTs.

REMEMBER

To be sure you adhere to tax and other regulatory laws, hire a tax professional who can help you with your particular situation.

3

Developing Your Knowledge: A Step-by-Step Guide to Programming Your Own NFT

Chapter **6**

What Is Ethereum?

I n this chapter, we provide a high-level overview of Ethereum: the platform from which so many tokens — both fungible and non-fungible — have spawned.

You don't need the information in this chapter in order to implement our step-by-step guide to minting your very own non-fungible ERC-721 token on the Ethereum platform. (These practical details and instructions begin in Chapter 7 and culminate in the creation of your very own NFT in Chapter 11.) However, this chapter provides useful information to help you better understand the basic features of your NFT and how it interacts with the rest of the Ethereum universe.

Revealing the Ethereum Virtual Machine

Imagine a single, all-powerful computer that stores and executes code based on the consensus of a leaderless community, also known as a *decentralized autonomous organization* (DAO). Computing power to process requests is paid for with fungible tokens (the native currency of this leaderless community), and community members who provide computational resources are compensated with these tokens. Anyone is free to enter and exit the community — no need to ask for permission — and members of the community can participate to the extent they desire.

Any member of the community can submit a request to the system, although each request must be paid for. For a request to be accepted, the community as a whole has to reach a consensus on whether the request is valid. To determine that validity, the community might ask the following questions:

>> Does the member in question have the required number of tokens to pay for the request?

>> Is the request feasible, given the resources of the community supercomputer?

>> Does this member have permission to make such a request?

For full transparency, all information (code, transactions, and token holdings, for example) is forever memorialized and accessible to all. To uphold the integrity of the state of this computer, each member of the community separately and continuously maintains updated copies of the system.

In the Ethereum universe, this computer is the *Ethereum Virtual Machine* (EVM), and the leaderless community is a network of computers operated by (literally!) anyone who wishes to participate. Each of these computers (also known as *nodes*) stores updated duplicates of the EVM. Anyone may additionally choose to participate as a *mining node,* or *miner,* who is compensated to validate and process computing requests for execution. The software itself is open source and free, though the necessary hardware and electricity are not.

To initiate a computing request, referred to as a *transaction*, you need an account that can receive, store, and send ether *(ETH)*, the native cryptocurrency of Ethereum. (These accounts can also deploy and interact with deployed smart contracts.) On Ethereum, this type of account is officially known as an *externally owned account*. When you hear someone mention accounts, they're likely referring to externally owned accounts.

In Chapter 7, we explain account types, account creation, and account management in greater detail.

REMEMBER

All transactions on the EVM must be paid for with ETH. Transactions can entail operations such as

>> Transferring ETH from one account to another

>> Storing data on the EVM

>> Manipulating existing data

After a requested transaction has been validated and executed — a process that requires network consensus — the new state of the EVM is broadcast and duplicated across the network of nodes. The entire history of transactions is secured on a blockchain-based distributed ledger for anyone to access.

To see how this public ledger works in practice, carry out the following steps to view all transactions data on the EVM since the genesis of the Ethereum blockchain:

1. **Go to** https://etherscan.io.

2. **Select the View Txns option from the Blockchain drop-down menu, as shown in Figure 6-1.**

There, for all the world to see, are all transactions data on the EVM since time immemorial.

Txns is Ethereum's bizarre way of referring to transactions.

TECHNICAL
STUFF

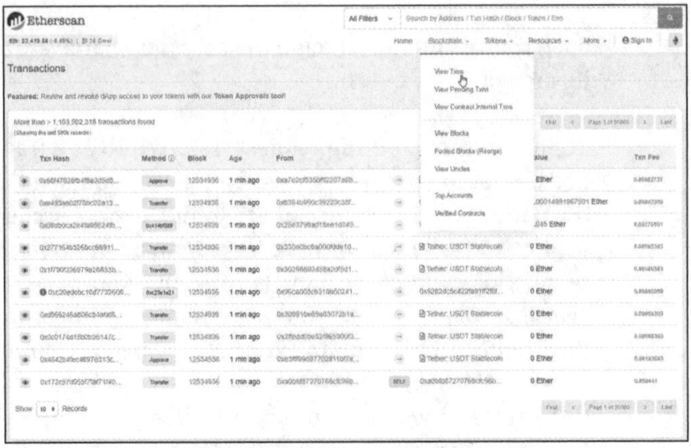

FIGURE 6-1:
Viewing transactions data on the Ethereum blockchain.

Ether: The Gas That Fuels Your Transactions

In Ethereum, *gas* is the unit of measurement used to denote the amount of computational work required to process a transaction on the EVM.

When you submit a transaction to the Ethereum network, you must designate two cost-related inputs:

>> **Gas price:** The price, in ETH, that you're willing to pay per unit of gas consumed by your transaction. Higher gas prices make your transaction more attractive to miners, who are compensated to validate and execute transactions.

>> **Gas limit:** The maximum total units of gas you're willing to consume to fully execute your transaction. Higher gas limits ensure that your transaction's computational needs are sufficiently covered for completion.

In general, the speed and successful execution of your request depends on the gas price and gas limit that you designate.

Depending on your wallet service and settings, you may notice that gas is denoted in *gwei*, where 1 million gwei is equal to 1 ETH.

TECHNICAL STUFF

The journey of a transaction

To help you better understand the overall likelihood of, and costs associated with, executing a transaction, here's a look at what happens when you initiate a request from your account:

1. Your transaction is assigned a unique code known as the transaction hash (and abbreviated as TxnHash, TxHash, or TXID).

    For illustrative purposes, here's an example of a TxnHash:

    0x7b91d4f49ccafdb93f2ca89fd57649301331b-d691cfe26478822afb468ac9589

2. The transaction is broadcast to the greater Ethereum network of nodes.

3. If valid, the transaction is added to a pool of other pending transactions awaiting execution.

    This pool (shown in Figure 6-2) is called the *mempool.* To see the details of a pending transaction, click the TxnHash. (See Figure 6-3.)

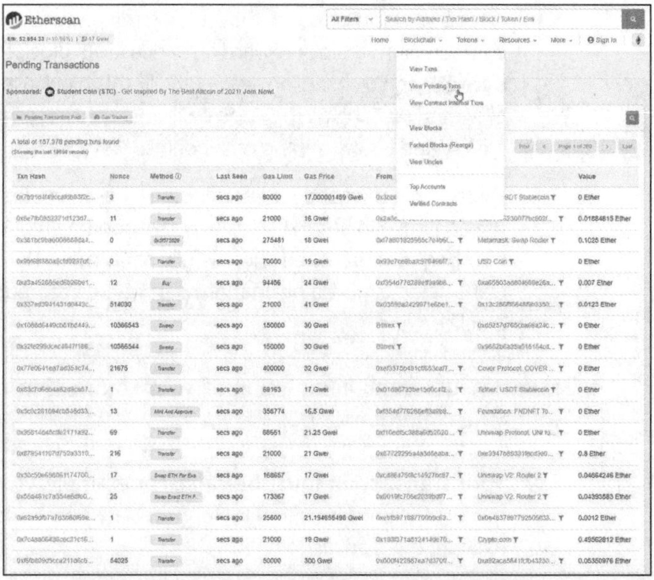

FIGURE 6-2: Unconfirmed transactions waiting in the mempool.

FIGURE 6-3: A pending transaction, awaiting confirmation and execution.

⑦ Transaction Hash:	0x7b91d4f49ccafdb93f2ca89fd576493013315d691cfe26478822afb468ac9589 ⧉
⑦ Status:	⚙ Pending
⑦ Block:	(Pending)
⑦ Time Last Seen:	⟳ 00 days 00 hr 00 min 07 secs ago (Jun-01-2021 06:50:54 AM)
⑦ Estimated Confirmation Duration:	< 9 mins	⛽ Gas Tracker
⑦ Pending Txn Queue: 🔘	0% ▬▬▬▬▬▬▬▬▬▬▬▬▬▬▬ 100%
⑦ From:	0x3bb63a4942d9c11498a18151264dde905806286b ⧉
⑦ Interacted With (To):	Contract 0xdac17f958d2ee523a2206206994597c13d831ec7 (Tether: USDT Stablecoin) ⧉
⑦ Token Transfer:	▸ Pending Transfer to ➝ 0xccbe19c71671410888... For 64 ♦ ERC-20 (Tether USD Token)
⑦ Value:	0 Ether ($0.00)
⑦ Max Txn Cost/Fee:	0.00136000011672 Ether ($3.61)
⑦ Gas Price:	0.000000017000001459 Ether (17.000001459 Gwei)

4. Mining nodes select pending transactions from this pool to form a (not-yet-confirmed) block of transactions.

(For reasons we discuss further below, miners tend to select pending transactions with higher gas prices.)

5. Miners race to solve a complex equation — a *proof-of-work (PoW) puzzle*, which requires vast computing power — to earn the right to add and confirm a new block to the Ethereum blockchain.

6. After a solution is found, the winning miner, who is compensated a block reward, broadcasts its block to the network, the transactions selected for this block are executed (as long as they don't exhaust their respective gas limits), and a new mining race begins.

Figure 6-4 shows the earlier pending transaction (introduced above in Step 1), with its corresponding block number, that has been successfully confirmed. This transaction is now a permanent part of the Ethereum blockchain.

Overall, successful completion of your transaction requires the following conditions:

>> **Your transaction must be valid.** For example, you must have sufficient funds and the appropriate permissions to execute the transaction.

FIGURE 6-4: Confirmation of the pending transaction from Figure 6-3.

>> **Your transaction must be confirmed and queued for execution.** Your transaction must be selected by a successful mining node that earns the right to append and confirm a new block to the Ethereum blockchain.

>> **Your transaction's total computational complexity must not exceed its designated gas limit.** (You, as the person requesting the transaction, set the gas limit.)

Compensating the (proof-of-) workers: What's in it for the miners?

For each new block added, the winning miner is paid a block reward, which comes in two parts:

>> **Fixed payment:** At the time of this writing, this fixed portion was 2 ETH.

>> **Individual fees:** These fees are attached to each transaction selected for the block in question.

For instance, the miner of Block #12546760 (see Figure 6-5) was compensated approximately 2.32175 ETH. This total block reward is broken down like this:

>> **2 ETH:** The fixed portion of the block reward

>> **0.32175 ETH:** The sum of the individual fees for each of the 236 transactions selected for this block

FIGURE 6-5: Metadata for Block #12546760.

⑦ Block Height:	12546760 ⟨ ⟩
⑦ Timestamp:	ⓘ 15 mins ago (Jun-01-2021 05:38:15 AM +UTC)
⑦ Transactions:	236 transactions and 34 contract internal transactions in this block
⑦ Mined by:	0x52bc44d5378309ee2abf1539bf71de1b7d7be3b5 (**Nanopool**) in 4 secs
⑦ Block Reward:	2.321750465869280353 Ether (2 + 0.321750465869280353)
⑦ Uncles Reward:	0
⑦ Difficulty:	7,575,898,402,191,356
⑦ Total Difficulty:	25,572,659,330,806,195,893,138
⑦ Size:	70,763 bytes
⑦ Gas Used:	14,976,460 (99.94%)
⑦ Gas Limit:	14,985,259
⑦ Extra Data:	nanopool.org (Hex:0x6e616e6f706f6f6c2e6f7267)

Naturally, miners want to maximize their potential compensation for a given amount of work: namely, the computing power they expend attempting to solve computationally taxing proof-of-work puzzles.

The difficulty level of these puzzles isn't impacted by the size or content of the latest block a miner is working to confirm. So, when selecting transactions for a block, miners are generally incentivized to select

» As many transactions as possible, adhering to the total gas limit imposed by Ethereum at the block level

» Transactions with the highest gas price per unit of gas

In turn, you can use this incentive scheme to decide how to set gas prices when you submit transactions to the network.

From happy hour to surge pricing: Determining a reasonable gas price

Higher gas prices are more attractive to miners when they're selecting transactions for their next block. Setting a higher gas price, as shown in Figure 6-6, improves the expected speed for your transaction to be selected, confirmed, and executed.

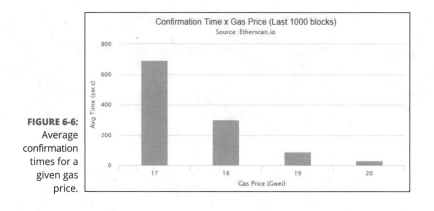

FIGURE 6-6: Average confirmation times for a given gas price.

How much should you offer to pay? After all, if you're not in a rush, you might prefer to pay less and wait on standby. In a moment of desperation, you might gladly pay $100 for a bottle of water in Death Valley and then regret the purchase if you hear a less desperate customer haggle the price down to $50.

The problem is that miners are happy to enjoy higher gas prices and to collect greater fees when offered. They won't tell you if they'd be willing to select your transaction at a lower price, and they certainly won't refund the difference. So how much should you commit to pay, given the level of urgency or lack thereof? And how should this amount differ when the network is quiet as opposed to when it's extremely congested?

TIP

Fortunately, many services, including MetaMask (which we cover in Chapter 2 and Chapter 4), provide guidance for novice users who can simply select Slow, Average, or Fast to automatically populate a transaction's gas price based on the wallet's internal algorithms. More advanced users can still choose to set a customized gas price using their own predictive analytics based on information gleaned from recently confirmed blocks.

For a quick and fun way to monitor recommended gas prices throughout the day, check out the ETH Gas Station at https://ethgasstation.info. Figure 6-7 shows gas prices captured at 10-minute intervals.

Etherscan has its own Ethereum Gas Tracker, shown in Figure 6-8, which can be accessed at https://etherscan.io/gastracker.

FIGURE 6-7: Snapshots of recommended gas prices from ETH Gas Station.

FIGURE 6-8: Etherscan's Ethereum Gas Tracker.

Setting your budget: Is the sky the (gas) limit?

Though a transaction's gas price impacts its expected speed of execution, the gas limit determines whether the transaction is even executed. What this means is that underfunded transactions ultimately fail to complete execution.

Since allotting sufficient gas to a transaction is important, you might naturally ask yourself the following two questions:

» What's wrong with simply setting the gas limit to an arbitrarily high amount?

» Can you calculate the required units of gas in advance to set an appropriate gas limit?

To address the first question, you can't rely on simply picking a large number for the gas limit, for a variety of reasons. Feasibility is a big one because

>> **The gas limit you can set for your transaction is constrained by the amount of ETH in your account.** You must have a balance higher than the transaction's gas price times the gas limit in order to submit the transaction.

>> **The gas limit on your transaction is also constrained by the prevailing block-level gas limit.** Your transaction cannot be included in a block if its gas limit exceeds the existing block-level gas limit.

Also, miners are less likely to select transactions with improbably large gas limits:

>> **The block-level gas limit constrains how many transactions a miner can select for a new block.**

>> **Miners are only compensated for the actual gas required to execute a transaction.** The unused gas within each transaction's allocated limit is returned to the originating account.

>> **Transactions that appear to grossly overshoot their gas limits are less desirable to miners.** The reason is that they occupy valuable block space without providing the commensurate compensation.

TIP

To address the second question, you can calculate the required units of gas, in advance, to set a reasonable gas limit for certain types of transactions. For simple transactions, such as transferring ETH from one account to another, the total gas required is clear before the execution. Consider a simple transfer with a cost of 21,000 units of gas. For this request, don't overthink the transaction's gas limit. Just set the gas limit to 21,000.

The total computational cost required to execute more complex requests, however, is often difficult to assess until after the transaction has been completed. The transaction may contain faulty but expensive loops or may be unintentionally complex in other ways.

REMEMBER

When submitting a transaction that entails more complex tasks, such as participating in an initial coin offering (ICO), your best bet is to start with guidance from the issuers. If you're the author of more complex functions that are being called, the best practice is to provide guidance to end users regarding how to set gas limits.

We discuss gas usage in more detail, with practical examples and tips, in Chapter 9 and in Chapter 11, where we show you how to code your own NFT on Ethereum.

Transaction fees

After your transaction has been confirmed and executed, the total transaction fee you incur (in ETH) is equal to the actual amount of gas used by the transaction times the gas price you designated.

REMEMBER

During the execution process, if your transaction's computational complexity exceeds its designated gas limit, your transaction won't successfully complete. However, you must still pay a fee equal to the gas limit times the gas price you designated because attempted executions still consume computing power on the EVM.

To see this concept in action, we look at the transaction fee for two different scenarios: one for a successful transaction and another for a transaction that runs out of gas.

Scenario 1: Transaction successfully executes

Consider a transaction submitted with the following inputs:

>> **Gas price:** 0.000000018 ETH

>> **Gas limit:** 437,603

After completion, the total actual gas used by this transaction was 307,804 units, which is less than the gas limit of 437,603.

The transaction successfully executes, as shown in Figure 6-9, and the total transaction fee incurred is

307,804 (gas used) * 0.000000018 ETH (gas price) =
0.005540472 ETH

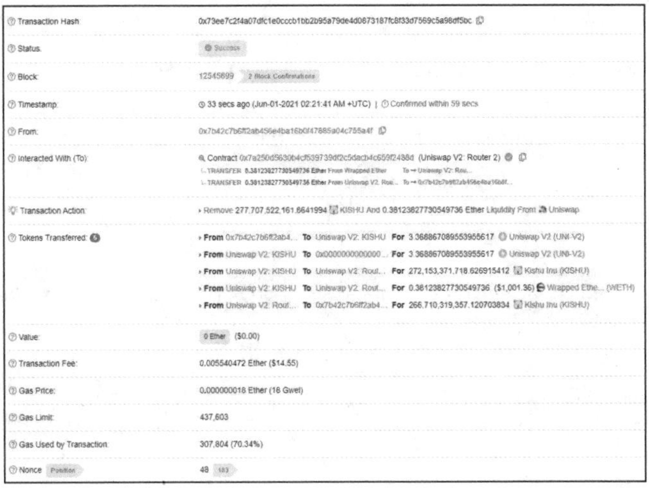

FIGURE 6-9:

FIGURE 6-9:
Gas consumption and the fee for a successful transaction.

Because this transaction didn't require the entire gas limit to complete, the remaining funds are returned to the originating account — this list explains the sequence of events:

>> At the outset, 437,603 (gas limit) * 0.000000018 ETH (gas price) = **0.007876854 ETH** is collected from the originating account, in anticipation of paying for the computing power required to execute this transaction.

>> Based on the actual gas consumed by the transaction, the miner is compensated a transaction fee in the amount of **0.005540472 ETH.**

>> The originating account is refunded the unused portion: 0.007876854 - 0.005540472 = **0.002336382 ETH.**

>> Because the transaction has been successfully executed, the state of the EVM has been altered and is rebroadcast to the network.

Scenario 2: Transaction runs out of gas

Consider another transaction submitted with the following inputs:

>> **Gas price:** 0.000025 ETH

>> **Gas limit:** 25,000

In this case, during execution, the miner discovers that the transaction's computational complexity exceeds its designated gas limit of 25,000, and the transaction runs out of gas (see Figure 6-10). The transaction won't be executed, but the total transaction fee incurred is

25,000 (gas limit) * 0.000025 ETH (gas price) = **0.625 ETH**

FIGURE 6-10: Gas consumption and the fee for an unsuccessful transaction.

⑦ Transaction Hash:	0xda8c0b80d8e240a63c8f6b067c4656babeb13e8e0ece4fd4292aa06252f1285c 🗐
⑦ Block:	3840222 8711411 Block Confirmations
⑦ Timestamp:	⏱ 1454 days 9 hrs ago (Jun-08-2017 02:02:57 PM +UTC)
⑦ From:	0xec5765df3b6a36ee32b9c4051d3eaec30f3f483 🗐
⑦ To:	Contract 0xace62f87abe9f4ee9fd6e115d91548df24ca0943 (Monaco: Token Sale) ⚠ 🗐 ∟ Warning! Error encountered during contract execution [Out of gas] ⊗
⑦ Value:	0.1 Ether ($264.13) → [CANCELLED] ❶
⑦ Transaction Fee:	0.625 Ether ($1,950.82)
⑦ Gas Price:	0.000025 Ether (25,000 Gwei)
⑦ Ether Price:	$259.41 / ETH
⑦ Gas Limit:	25,000
⑦ Gas Used by Transaction:	25,000 (100%)

Although this transaction failed to execute, the miner must still be compensated for the computing work provided:

>> At the outset, 25,000 (gas limit) * 0.000025 ETH (gas price) = **0.625 ETH** is collected from the originating account.

>> Based on the computing power used by the miner in its (unsuccessful) efforts to execute this transaction, the miner is compensated a transaction fee in the amount of **0.625 ETH**.

> » Because the transaction wasn't executed, the state of the EVM remains as it was before the attempted execution.
>
> » No funds remain to be transferred back to the originating account.

What a shame to pay 0.625 ETH for nothing to happen!

REMEMBER

The total amount you can be charged for your transaction is capped by the gas price times the gas limit you designate. If your transaction is executed at a lower cost, the gas price times unused gas is returned to your account.

The Blockchain: Where It's All Stored and Secured

All confirmed transactions on the EVM are forever memorialized on the Ethereum blockchain — a blockchain-based distributed ledger that acts as a permissionless and shared database synchronized across multiple nodes. Any of the nodes can access the ledger, and updates are copied to all nodes (nearly) simultaneously. The blockchain entails a recordkeeping system that organizes information into chronological blocks of data — in other words, transaction records are grouped into blocks that are regularly confirmed and appended to the existing chain.

Each block is linked to the block preceding it by including a hash of the prior block's information, forming a *blockchain*. Blocks are often referenced by block height, which represents a block's location in the blockchain — or, equivalently, the number of blocks preceding it. The *genesis* block is referenced as block 0.

Each newly formed block requires network consensus before it can be added to the ever-growing chain of confirmed blocks. As always, miners furiously race to solve a computationally taxing puzzle to earn the right to append their block to the existing blockchain. The solution to this puzzle, known as proof of work, is difficult to produce but easy to confirm. For instance, guessing someone's phone number is an onerous task, but you can easily confirm that you have the correct solution when the phone number is given to you.

When miners reach a solution, they close out the pending block and broadcast the results to the rest of the network, the blockchain is updated, and then a new speed race begins to confirm the next block.

Ethash and proof of work: What makes Ethereum tamper-proof?

Public blockchains, such as those of Ethereum and Bitcoin, require a consensus mechanism to ensure that the system is

>> **Fault tolerant:** The system should continue to operate, even in the presence of faulty, failed, or malicious nodes.

>> **Secure:** The rules governing how the network collectively confirms and agrees on the status of the ledger should ensure that, even if there exists a group of dishonest nodes, the records remain tamper-proof.

The consensus mechanism securing the Ethereum blockchain is predicated on a proof-of-work algorithm known as Ethash (though developers are working to move the system to a proof-of-stake consensus mechanism). Because proof of work requires solving a long and onerous problem to confirm and execute transactions, closed blocks of information are difficult to alter, because a dishonest node must laboriously and painstakingly find a solution to a new puzzle based on the altered information.

Because proof-of-work systems are, by design, computationally cumbersome, participants have expressed mounting concerns over the energy consumption and environmental unfriendliness of cryptocurrencies whose security protocols depend on proof of work. Companies (see Figure 6-11) as well as countries (see Figure 6-12) are changing attitudes about cryptocurrency payments and cryptomining. In response, consensus mechanisms based on proof-of-stake (PoS) protocols are increasingly popular. In contrast to proof of work, *proof of stake* requires sufficient stake — measured by factors such as account balance or account age—in the system to confirm transactions.

Elon Musk @elonmusk

Tesla & Bitcoin

Tesla has suspended vehicle purchases using Bitcoin. We are concerned about rapidly increasing use of fossil fuels for Bitcoin mining and transactions, especially coal, which has the worst emissions of any fuel.

Cryptocurrency is a good idea on many levels and we believe it has a promising future, but this cannot come at great cost to the environment.

Tesla will not be selling any Bitcoin and we intend to use it for transactions as soon as mining transitions to more sustainable energy. We are also looking at other cryptocurrencies that use <1% of Bitcoin's energy/transaction.

3:06 PM · May 12, 2021 · Twitter for iPhone

FIGURE 6-11: Elon Musk tweets concerns about the sustainability of crypto-mining.

CRYPTOCURRENCY

Major bitcoin mining region in China sets tough penalties for cryptocurrency activities

PUBLISHED TUE, MAY 25 2021·11:12 PM EDT | UPDATED WED, MAY 26 2021·10:56 AM EDT

Arjun Kharpal
@ARJUNKHARPAL

CRYPTOCURRENCY

Iran bans bitcoin mining as its cities suffer blackouts and power shortages

PUBLISHED WED, MAY 26 2021·2:27 PM EDT | UPDATED WED, MAY 26 2021·2:39 PM EDT

Natasha Turak
@NATASHATURAK

SHARE f 𝕏 in ✉

FIGURE 6-12: Crackdowns on crypto-mining activity in the news.

For years, the Ethereum community has been anticipating Ethereum 2.0, a shift from the current system based on proof of work to one that's based on proof of stake. Although plenty of speculation takes place around a possible move to Ethereum 2.0 in the near future, as of this writing, proof of work remains the prevailing authority.

Miners and nonces and bears — oh, my!

The "proof" of a successful miner's proof of work lies in the block nonce included in the block header. (The block header contains important information about each confirmed block.)

The curiously named *block nonce* is a number that can be found only by way of a computationally intense process of trial-and-error. In this process, miners continually try arbitrary values until they find the special number — the nonce — that, when combined with other important elements of the current block, satisfies a mathematical condition required by the Ethash protocol. Thus, this nonce is difficult to find but easy to verify after a solution is announced.

The required mathematical condition is a moving target based on the current block's difficulty level. Block difficulty is dynamically adjusted based on the previous block's difficulty level and recent block times. The new difficulty level could be greater than or less than the previous block's level, a dynamic adjustment ensuring that blocks aren't formed too quickly or too slowly for a prolonged period as miners enter and exit the network.

WARNING

Don't confuse the block nonce with the *transaction nonce,* a number denoting a chronological ordering of transactions sent from a given account.

How many "confirmations" until I'm actually confirmed?

The most recent block is the most vulnerable to attacks because no blocks follow it, removing the need to resolve numerous proof-of-work puzzles. A malicious group of nodes can collude to launch what is known as a *51% attack,* assembling at least half the network's computing power. Their end goal would be to spend the same funds twice (known as *double-spending*). This group might employ the following strategy:

1. Submit a transaction to send ETH to an account at a cryptoexchange.

2. Upon block confirmation and execution, immediately convert the ETH to USD and withdraw the funds.

3. At the same time, reverse the transaction from Step 1, by exploiting the group's collective computing power to swiftly find a new proof-of-work solution that fits with the now-altered block.

4. Repeat.

However, even with sufficient computing power to re-solve and alter the contents of the most recently closed block, this group would be hard-pressed to re-solve and alter 50 blocks quickly enough to override the previous network consensus that confirmed those blocks.

To counter these types of attacks, vendors and wallet services typically require that confirmed transactions be numerous blocks deep before considering the transaction to be truly confirmed. The number of confirmations required before pending funds are credited to your account varies across cryptocurrencies and across different vendors and wallet services. Figure 6-13 shows the number of confirmations required as well as the estimated wait times for a select subset of cryptocurrencies on Kraken, a major US cryptoexchange.

Kraken's confirmations requirements		
Cryptocurrency	Confirmations Required	Estimated Time* If included in the next block.
Bitcoin (BTC)	4 confirmations	EST 40 minutes Dependent on Fee
Bitcoin Cash (BCH)	15 confirmations	2.5 hours (150 minutes)
Cardano (ADA)	15 confirmations	10 minutes
Chainlink (LINK)	20 confirmations	5 minutes
Ethereum (ETH)	20 confirmations	5 minutes
Ethereum Classic (ETC)	40,000 confirmations	6.5 days

FIGURE 6-13: Kraken's confirmations required and estimated wait times.

Kraken now requires Ethereum transactions to be 20 blocks deep (that's 20 confirmations) before making the funds available for trading or withdrawal. In contrast, Coinbase requires 35 confirmations, and Gemini requires only 12.

Uncles and orphans

Given the vast network of mining nodes competing to form new blocks, you'll end up with simultaneous or near-simultaneous proof-of-work solutions. In these cases, the network sees two new blocks created and appended at the same block height — also known as the *block number* — causing a temporary split in the blockchain. More accurately, as the dueling results are broadcast to the network, one result will reach some nodes first while the other result reaches other nodes. For a brief moment, different nodes have different versions of the state of the blockchain.

As the next speed race ensues, one chain prevails as subsequent blocks are confirmed and appended. This means the network ultimately accepts the chain involving more work (typically, the longer chain), and only one of the dueling blocks remains confirmed by the network while the other becomes stale.

The stale block in this scenario is called an *uncle block* in Ethereum-speak (represented graphically in Figure 6-14). Uncle blocks are also referred to as *ommer blocks*, which is the gender-neutral equivalent. In the Bitcoin universe, these blocks are called *orphan blocks*.

FIGURE 6-14: A temporary split in the blockchain results in an uncle block.

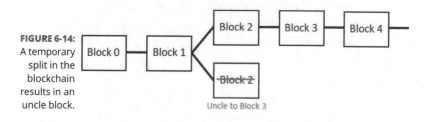

Hard forks: Updates to the underlying protocol

In DAOs like Ethereum, participants are free to enter and exit the network whenever they want and to involve themselves to the extent they desire, so anyone can choose to do any of the following:

>> View the entire history of transactions.

>> Maintain a replica of the state of the EVM.

>> Participate as a miner working to confirm and add new blocks to the chain.

In addition, the general Ethereum community manages patches and updates to the underlying *network protocol* — the system of code and rules that govern Ethereum. Anyone in the community is free to propose updates to the underlying protocol by submitting an *Ethereum improvement proposal* (EIP). Ultimately, a group of the most involved and significant contributors to protocol development, known as *Ethereum core developers*, collectively determines which EIPs to implement.

Major changes require a *fork* to the underlying consensus protocol, forcing a permanent split to the blockchain so that all subsequent blocks appended along the forked path must follow the new consensus protocol. Typically, hard forks to the Ethereum blockchain have not resulted in new (fungible) tokens, because the community generally follows the direction of the core developers. Accordingly, the prong operating under the older protocol typically dies a quiet death simply from lack of activity.

TECHNICAL
STUFF

The most notable and controversial exception to this general trend of harmonious forking involves a hard fork to the Ethereum blockchain in 2016, which resulted in a major rift within the community and, accordingly, two separate tokens: ETH and ETC (Ethereum Classic).

Smart Contracts Make the EVM Go Round

A *smart contract* is a software program that, once deployed, is housed in a special contract account with its own, unique address on the EVM. The act of deploying a smart contract is itself a transaction and requires gas. (We introduce smart contracts in Chapter 2, and we show you how to code and deploy your own smart contract in Chapter 9.)

Once deployed, smart contracts lie dormant until triggered by a transaction. Many transactions on the Ethereum blockchain are designed to call functions housed in various smart contracts, which may in turn trigger calls to other smart contract functions. (See Figure 6-15.) A *function* in this context is a self-contained piece of code written to accomplish a specific task. A *call* references a function located elsewhere — in this case, in other smart contracts.

FIGURE 6-15:
A sample transaction, initiating a call to a smart contract function.

Smart contracts are designed to enforce a set of rules that are automatically executed when called. A carefully designed smart contract, by way of the EVM, is programmed to enforce agreements by verifying desired conditions and initiating subsequent computing requests or data updates accordingly. And it all happens without needing a trusted intermediary!

WARNING

As with any application coming from an unknown or untrusted source, you should exercise caution when engaging with smart-contract applications on Ethereum.

The nascent life of a smart contract

Suppose you want to deploy a smart contract to raise ETH for a new fund. For instance, Blockchain Capital (a venture capital firm in San Francisco) raised $10 million through a BCAP token offering, which was implemented as a smart contract on Ethereum. Here's what that process looks like:

1. You submit a transaction containing your compiled code, specifying the appropriate gas price and gas limit for execution.

2. When your transaction has been confirmed and executed, your contract account is created and assigned an address.

3. Shortly thereafter, a potential investor submits a transaction to initiate a call to your smart contract's deposit function.

4. Once a miner has selected this transaction and confirmed the block, the transaction begins execution and your smart contract's deposit function is called.

5. The deposit function, in turn, calls another internal function to confirm whether the potential investor meets your fund's investor criteria — say, minimum ETH deposit and minimum age of account.

6. If these conditions are satisfied, the deposit function accepts the ETH deposit.

7. Assuming that the investor has designated an adequate gas limit, the transaction is fully executed and the state of the EVM is updated.

Take a bow! You've managed to deploy an application that enables you to raise capital for your fund in an automated fashion with a secure validation process that is both decentralized and autonomous!

In Chapter 9, we provide the actual step-by-step guide to write, compile, and deploy your own Ethereum smart contract.

Exciting possibilities

A new kid on the block(chain) that's increasingly in vogue comes in the form of *decentralized applications* (*dApps*) — or apps that run on aa blockchain. Their allure stems from a desire to both democratize finance and cut out the middlemen. Their attractiveness is also due to the popularity of cryptocurrencies and their skyrocketing value. If you think of Ethereum as a decentralized Internet – what many refer to as Web3 or Web 3.0, then dApps are the decentralized websites in this system.

Numerous dApps on the EVM are built for many different purposes. For instance, smart contracts can be designed to do any of the following (although one contract wouldn't necessarily do *all* of these things):

>> Execute an ICO.

>> Generate and support fungible tokens (that is, cryptocurrencies).

>> Create and trade non-fungible collectibles (that is, NFTs).

>> Provide a decentralized social media outlet.

- >> Conduct a decentralized exchange.
- >> Host a decentralized betting market.

Notable limitations

The EVM is a *closed system*, meaning everything on Ethereum is entirely self-contained, which ensures that consensus about the true state of the EVM is never jeopardized. Every node in the Ethereum network must be able to linearly execute all confirmed transactions — from the originating block to the most recent block — and reach the same conclusion regarding each block-dependent state of the EVM up through its most recent state (for example, live accounts, account balances, active smart contracts, and data stored).

Depending on information outside of this system could lead to glitches that can short-circuit a contract's successful completion. Suppose that a smart contract's next steps depend on the dollar value of an account's ETH balance rather than on the ETH balance itself. The randomness inherent in obtaining the off-chain USD/ETH exchange rate violates how smart contracts must execute orders. The results might be different based on when a node queries the off-chain information to determine the transition from one state of the EVM to the next.

REMEMBER

Ultimately, this means that smart contracts can issue calls to other functions only within the contract itself or in other smart contracts on the EVM. They cannot send HTTP requests to transfer data (such as when you access information on the Internet) or interact with external (off-chain) application programming interfaces (APIs), which could compromise consensus across nodes.

Oracles: How to Connect to the "Outside" World

Suppose you want to develop a betting app on the EVM that is designed to send ETH to certain accounts if the temperature in San Francisco exceeds 100 degrees at any time on January 1,

2025, as reported by www.weather.com. Because you can't program smart contracts to send message requests for information outside of the Ethereum blockchain, you need a clever way to get this off-chain information to your smart contract in a reliable and automated fashion. Enter oracles.

Oracles provide a way to send structured, up-to-date information to the EVM. In the weather-betting example, you can develop a separate off-chain application to do the following:

1. Submit HTTP requests to www.weather.com beginning at 12:00:00 A.M. on January 1, 2025.

2. If the reported temperature in San Francisco exceeds 100 degrees, have your off-chain application submit a transaction to the Ethereum network, requesting to send this information to the smart contract address housing your on-chain betting app.

3. Once this transaction is mined and executed, the confirmed over-100-degree status triggers your on-chain betting app to initiate ETH fund transfers to the appropriate accounts.

REMEMBER

Any oracle is only as reliable and secure as its data sources and programming logic. As more complex blockchain apps increase in number and popularity, so has the demand for oracle services. Such services provide the infrastructure to access common off-chain data and computations, such as in these examples:

>> **Random-number generation for blockchain games:** *CryptoKitties* was the first widely used blockchain game, though now you can find several others. See Chapter 2 for more about *CryptoKitties.*

>> **Price feeds for betting, or DeFi, apps:** DeFi stands for *de*centralized *fi*nance, a system offering financial services on a public, decentralized blockchain network.

>> **Data feeds from other public blockchains:** Bitcoin and Litecoin are examples of other public blockchains.

Here are a few popular oracle services:

- **Chainlink:** `https://chain.link`
- **Provable:** `https://provable.xyz`
- **Witnet:** `https://witnet.io`

Shining a Light on Ethereum's Fundamental Structure

This section revisits terms and concepts discussed throughout this chapter, presented here with their interdependent relations.

The big picture

These keywords are an essential part of your Ethereum repertoire. Any conversation about Ethereum in particular, and crypto in general, invariably involves these terms:

- **Ethereum Virtual Machine (EVM):** A distributed computing platform where participating nodes store updated duplicates of the state of the EVM

- **Ether (ETH):** Ethereum's native token

  All computing requests on the EVM require sufficient ETH to execute.

- **Blockchain:** A recordkeeping system in which transaction records are grouped into chronologically ordered blocks, with each block cryptographically linked to the block preceding it

- **Distributed ledger:** A public and permissionless recordkeeping system that's accessible to anyone who wants to participate without requiring permission from a central authority

>> **Decentralized autonomous organization (DAO):**
A leaderless organization that operates autonomously
and maintains consensus based on a nexus of rules and
open-source smart contracts

Nuts-and-bolts of the blockchain

Discussing the following technical concepts is a great way to flex
your crypto-prowess:

>> **Miner (mining node):** A specialized node that is compen-
sated to validate and process computing requests by
solving computationally taxing proof-of-work puzzles

>> **Consensus mechanism:** Provides the rules in place to
ensure that a decentralized network continues to operate
by being able to agree on correct information and to reject
false information in the face of dishonest participants in
the network

>> **Ethereum Improvement Proposal (EIP):** A proposal to
update aspects of the underlying protocol that governs
Ethereum

>> **Proof of work (PoW):** A security protocol that requires
participants to solve long and onerous puzzles to confirm
and execute transactions

>> **Proof of stake (PoS):** A security protocol that requires
participants to demonstrate sufficient stake in the system
to confirm and execute transactions

>> **Block height (block number):** Indicates a block's location
in the blockchain or, more accurately, the number of blocks
preceding it

The originating (or genesis) block is numbered as block 0.

>> **Block nonce:** Shows the successful miner's proof of work,
which satisfies a mathematical condition required by
Ethereum's PoW-based consensus protocol and allows the
miner to confirm and append the block to the growing
blockchain

>> **51% attack:** Occurs whenever a colluding group of miners amasses more than half the network's computing power in an attempt to game the system

>> **Uncle (ommer) block (also known by the gender-neutral term ommer block):** A now-stale block that was simultaneously mined alongside a valid block from which the Ethereum chain continues to grow

   Uncle blocks are known as *orphans* in the Bitcoin blockchain.

>> **Hard fork:** Entails a major change to the underlying consensus protocol, which forces a permanent split to the blockchain

   Hard forks to the Ethereum blockchain don't typically result in separate tokens.

Gas essentials

The words listed in this section might not be conventionally fun, but knowing their roles in a transaction's execution speed and success is essential for ultimate street cred:

>> **Transaction:** Represents a computing request on the EVM.

>> **Transaction hash (TxnHash):** The unique code assigned to each transaction.

>> **Gas price:** Represents how much ETH someone is willing to pay per unit of gas consumed by the submitted transaction.

>> **Gas limit:** Represents the maximum units of gas one is willing to use to fully execute the submitted transaction.

>> **Transaction fee:** The actual amount of gas used to execute the transaction times the gas price designated for the transaction.

Things that make the EVM an interesting place

Being able to chat about the following topics will bring added sparkle to your Ethereum conversations:

>> **Smart contract:** A set of code and data designed to enforce deterministic rules that are automatically executed when called.

>> **Decentralized application (dApps):** The programs running on the EVM.

>> **Oracle:** Provides a way to send off-chain information to the EVM.

Chapter **7**

Creating an Ethereum Account

This chapter walks you through setting up different types of accounts on Ethereum and explains how to properly fund each one. Because this chapter covers the first critical step in the journey toward building your own ERC-721 non-fungible token, we recommend that you read the full chapter to understand the basic features we use and selections we make along the way. However, you *need* to read only the final section of this chapter, "Preparing Your Accounts (on MetaMask)," so feel free to skip straight to the end if you're in a rush.

REMEMBER

Before you dive into the hands-on instructions in this chapter, you must install and set up a MetaMask wallet. You also need some ETH funds in your account (especially if you plan to mint an actual NFT on the Ethereum network). We show you how to do both of these tasks in Chapter 2 and Chapter 4.

Understanding Externally Owned Accounts

Externally owned accounts (EOAs) are used to submit computing requests on the Ethereum network. An EOA can receive, store, and send ether (the native cryptocurrency of the Ethereum platform) as well as interact with deployed smart contracts. A request might be made to transfer funds from one EOA to another or to call functions in various smart contracts on the EVM — the Ethereum Virtual Machine, which we introduce in Chapter 6.

REMEMBER

EOAs are often simply referred to as *accounts,* and we follow the same convention. In fact, your first foray into creating an account on Ethereum — using MetaMask, which we cover in Chapters 2 and 4 — was indeed to create what's formally known as an externally owned account. Throughout this book, we use the terms *account* and *externally owned account* interchangeably.

Here are a few things to keep in mind:

>> You need an account to submit transactions on the Ethereum network.

>> Accounts can initiate transactions to interact with smart contracts or with other accounts.

>> Transactions between accounts can only be requests to transfer funds (ETH).

>> An account is not a wallet, and a wallet is not an account.

REMEMBER

Wallet services, such as MetaMask, are designed to help you manage your Ethereum accounts. Much like you can use different email clients to access emails sent to your email address, you can use different wallet services to access your Ethereum accounts.

Creating an account is simple and free. It doesn't cost any ETH to create an account, though you do need to fund your account before you can submit transactions, which — as we discuss in Chapter 6 — aren't always simple and certainly aren't free.

What it means to create an account

Many wallet services can create accounts for you. These services, such as MetaMask, are just generating key pairs:

>> **A private key:** You use your private key to access funds in your account, so you should never share your private key.

>> **A corresponding public address:** You can share your public address with other, so that you can receive funds from other accounts.

Of course, you don't need a wallet service to generate your key pairs for you. In fact, selecting a private key is as simple as picking a random number between 0 and 2^{256}, which is greater than 1 trillion to the power of 6 — or 1 trillion $\times$ 1 trillion $\times$ 1 trillion $\times$ 1 trillion $\times$ 1 trillion $\times$ 1 trillion.

Because there are so many possible private keys, even if all 8 billion people on Earth each created 1,000 accounts, the total number of active accounts — 8 trillion, in this scenario — would be far less than the total number of possible accounts. Guessing or generating a private key that's already being used is unlikely.

TECHNICAL STUFF

Still, having a wallet service do the heavy lifting has its benefits, especially if you aren't mathematically adept. Technically, you must pick a private key value greater than 0 and less than FFFFFFFFFFFFFFFFFFFFFFFFFFFFFFFFFFFFFFFFFEBAAEDCE6AF48A03BBF D25E8CD0364141 (which is less than the value of 2^{256}).

Private keys are expressed as 64-digit hexadecimal numbers, which is a base 16 notional system where each digit is represented by one of the following 16 characters: 0, 1, 2, 3, 4, 5, 6, 7, 8, 9, A, B, C, D, E, or F. For example:

>> 412 in hexadecimal is equal to $(4 \times 16^3) + (1 \times 16^2) + (2 \times 16^0)$ = 16,642 in decimal numbers, with which we're more familiar.

>> F9C3 in hexadecimal is equal to $(15 \times 16^4) + (9 \times 16^3) + (12 \times 16^2) + (3 \times 16^0)$ = 1,022,979 in decimal numbers.

TIP

As you process the calculations above, keep in mind that any number to the power of zero is equal to one.

After you randomly generate a private key, you need to generate a corresponding public key via an Elliptic Curve Digital Signature Algorithm (ECDSA). (Both Bitcoin and Ethereum use the secp256k1 ECDSA as their algorithm for public key generation.) After that, you still need to hash the resulting public key using the keccak256 hash function, take the last 40 hexadecimal digits (or last 20 bytes), and then add "0x" to the beginning to arrive at your public account address. See the later section "Digital signatures" to find out more about the mathematical algorithms used for authentication.

Private versus public keys

You use your private key to withdraw funds from your account; your public address is what you can publicly display to receive funds to your account. Of course, you must know your account's private keys if you want to access your accounts from a different wallet service that you haven't yet used to access those particular accounts.

To access your account's private key and public address on MetaMask, follow these steps:

1. **Log in to MetaMask.**

   Your account's name appears with its public address beneath it, as shown in Figure 7-1. In this case, the account name is NFTs For Dummies, and the public address is

   ```
   0xf77a3cE366E32645ffC78B9a88B7e90583646df9
   ```

2. **Click the account name to copy your public address.**

   The public address has 42 digits in hexadecimal notation (or 40 hexadecimal digits with a "0x" prefix added.

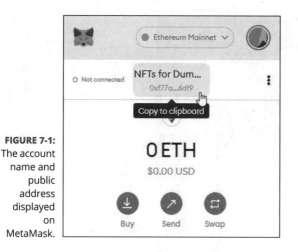

FIGURE 7-1:
The account
name and
public
address
displayed
on
MetaMask.

3. **Click the vertical ellipses to the right of the account name and choose Account Details from the drop-down menu, as shown in Figure 7-2.**

   The Account Details tab, shown in Figure 7-3, appears.

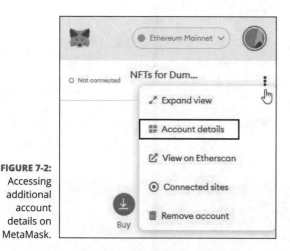

FIGURE 7-2:
Accessing
additional
account
details on
MetaMask.

4. **Click the Export Private Key button.**

5. **Enter your MetaMask wallet password and click Confirm, as shown in Figure 7-4.**

FIGURE 7-3:
The Account
Details
tab on
MetaMask.

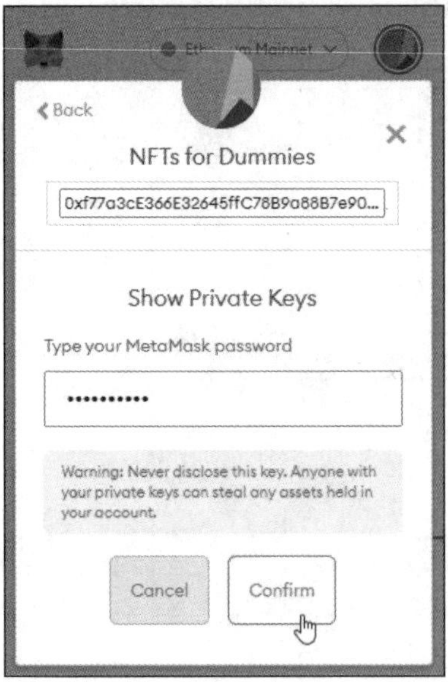

FIGURE 7-4:
Password
prompt to
access an
account's
private
key on
MetaMask.

6. Now you can simply click to copy the account's private key.

For the NFTs For Dummies account shown in Figure 7-5, we get the following private key, which is 64 digits in hexadecimal notation:

```
0bf71f18f67efa95140d5fe4c68afe06f9c9e475b0dde
    035d06a83d8026f441c
```

FIGURE 7-5:
An
account's
private key,
displayed
on
MetaMask.

< Back

NFTs for Dummies

Oxf77a3cE366E32645ffC78B9a88B7e90...

Show Private Keys

This is your private key (click to copy)

0bf71f18f67efa95140d5fe4c68afe0
6f9c9e475b0dde035d06a83d8026
f441c

Warning: Never disclose this key. Anyone with
your private keys can steal any assets held in
your account.

Done

Of course, do *not* announce your private key to the world (as we have just done here).

WARNING

Overall, private and public keys are used together to form a digital signature to validate a transaction. This process ensures that only the rightful account owner can submit transactions from a given account.

Digital signatures

How does the private/public key pair work to ensure that only you can spend the ETH in your account? By using *digital signatures*, which are mathematical algorithms that validate the authenticity of a digital message or document. Here, we provide a simple example of how digital signatures work. The basic elements are listed here:

- >> A single public key corresponds to each private key.

- >> Revealing your public key doesn't provide information about your private key.

- >> Your private key is combined with your public key and your transaction information to form a signature.

- >> This signature, along with your requested transaction, is broadcasted throughout the network.

- >> When validators apply your public key to the publicly broadcasted signature, they should get back the original transaction information.

TECHNICAL STUFF

Suppose that you have a private key, $Kpriv = \{7\}$, that only you know and a corresponding public key, $Kpub = \{3, 33\}$, that is shared with everyone. Also suppose that you want to send 16 ETH from this account.

The following steps show, in a simplified way, how digital signatures can work to prove that you're the rightful owner of the account in question:

1. **Take the number 16 (the amount you wish to send) to the power of 7 (your private key) and then divide by 33 (which is part of the public key).**

In other words, divide 167 by 33. The remainder of this division is equal to 25. This number, 25, which is your digital signature for this transaction, proves that you're the rightful account owner without revealing your private key.

2. **Submit your 16 ETH transfer request along with your digital signature of 25.**

That is, broadcast the pair of numbers $\{16, 25\}$ for verification.

3. **To verify that you're the rightful owner, validators apply your known public key $K_{pub} = \{3, 33\}$ by taking 25 to the power of 3 and then dividing by 33.**

The remainder of this division is exactly equal to 16, proving that you're the rightful owner.

From here, your transaction is added to a memory pool of pending transactions waiting to be added to the blockchain — all without disclosing your private key $K_{priv} = \{7\}$!

REMEMBER

If a malicious user tries to withdraw funds from your account, they can't do so without your private key. Suppose that the malicious user wrongly guesses that your private key is equal to $\{8\}$ (instead of the true $K_{priv} = \{7\}$). Here's what would happen:

1. To sign the 16 ETH transfer request, the malicious user now takes 16 to the power of 8 (instead of 7) and then divides by 33 (using the information in your public key $K_{pub} = \{3, 33\}$).

   The remainder here is now 4, which is the digital signature that is broadcast to the network.

2. The malicious user submits the transaction request along with the digital signature $\{16, 4\}$, claiming that they're the rightful owner and requesting to withdraw 16 ETH, with a digital signature proof of 4.

3. To verify, validators take 4 to the power of 3 and then divide by 33 (again, using the known public key $K_{pub} = \{3, 33\}$).

   The remainder of the division is 31, which doesn't equal the 16 ETH transfer request.

   Thus, this fraudulent transaction is rejected, demonstrating the beauty of digital signatures.

Of course, this simple example doesn't fully convey the digital signing and verification process that Ethereum uses. Still, it shows how key pairs and digital signatures operate to credibly demonstrate that you're the rightful owner of an account without ever disclosing your private keys.

Discovering Contract Accounts

REMEMBER

Contract accounts, which are often simply referred to as contracts or smart contracts, are designed to store data and code at a designated contract address on the EVM. In essence, when you deploy a software program to the EVM, you create a contract account that houses this program.

Contract accounts (contracts) differ from externally owned accounts (accounts) in several key ways:

>> **Contracts will cost you ETH.** The creation of a contract account is itself a transaction that must be initiated from an externally owned account.

>> **Contracts cannot initiate transactions.** Once created, contract accounts lie dormant until triggered by a transaction. A contract account can be called by another contract account, but this string of calls must ultimately originate from an externally owned account.

>> **Contracts have no private keys.** Contract accounts have only public addresses, which — like those of externally owned accounts — are also represented by a 42-digit hexadecimal number.

Naturally, because transactions cannot be initiated from a contract account, there's no need for contract accounts to have private keys.

After a contract has been deployed to the EVM, it is public and anyone can access it. Anyone is free to use the functions embedded in the contract or to even access all its source code, which can be found on the public blockchain as follows:

1. **Go to** https://etherscan.io.

2. **In the text-based search bar in the upper-right corner, type the address of the contract you want to find.**

3. **Click the Contract tab on the tab row across the top of the screen to see the contract's source code, as shown in Figure 7-6.**

   The contract address is

   ```
   0x1A79E50064C012639fB6fB6761E332Acf5Ba15d1
   ```

Although creating a contract account costs gas, after that contract account has been created, the creator pays no ongoing maintenance fees to keep the contract account up and running. Instead, anyone who wants to use functions embedded in the contract must initiate a request from an externally owned account and pay for the appropriate amount of gas for that transaction.

FIGURE 7-6:
Finding a
contract's
source
code.

Creating a contract account entails submitting a transaction that contains your code without specifying a destination address. In other words, you don't simply create a contract account without purpose in the way that you might simply create an externally owned account, even if you don't yet have a reason to use it.

TIP

The following list highlights important points about contract accounts (even though you aren't ready to do a lot of these things just yet):

>> To create a contract account, your smart-contract code should already be ready to go.

>> From an externally owned account, submit an Ethereum transaction to the network containing your compiled code without specifying any recipients.

>> Once validated and mined, your smart contract has its own public address on the Ethereum blockchain for future reference by anyone in the network.

Before you can create a contract account, you first need to follow the steps in the later section "Preparing Your Accounts (on MetaMask)" to set up your various (externally owned) accounts for different uses. After that, you must complete the steps of setting up your development environment (see Chapter 8) before proceeding to finally deploying your first smart contract (see Chapter 9).

Knowing the Difference Between Public Networks and Private Environments

Public networks are permissionless and open to anyone who wants to participate without requiring permission from a central authority. Two categories of public networks are important to the Ethereum ecosystem:

» **Mainnet:** This main Ethereum network is the primary blockchain on which transactions of actual value occur and are memorialized. When someone talks about Ethereum, Mainnet is generally what they're talking about. You need to use real, honest-to-goodness ETH to fuel transactions on Mainnet.

» **Testnets:** Test networks are available for developers to test various features before transacting on Mainnet. You get to use test-ETH — rather than the real thing — to fuel transactions on a testnet.

Even before playing around on a testnet, developers often test their code on a local development environment, which has the advantages of being faster and simpler.

Local development environments

Local development environments are private and provide an easy-and-safe sandbox where you can observe how your smart contracts might behave after they're deployed. *Sandboxes* are safe because they're isolated testing environments built for experimentation — the code in a sandbox isn't live, so errors don't cause real damage or network congestion.

These local environments, such as Ganache (which we introduce in Chapter 8), simulate the Ethereum blockchain by providing a private blockchain with preseeded test accounts. Unlike in a public network, your transactions are automatically executed in order to make it easier to debug your contracts without having to wait for blocks to be mined via an onerous proof-of-work process. (See Chapter 6 for an explanation of proof of work.)

Test networks

Public testnets provide another practice environment closer to how the main Ethereum network functions. Unlike local development environments, testnets provide public blockchains that mostly follow the rules of the main Ethereum blockchain.

Testnets provide a gateway to Ethereum without the pain of wasting actual ETH to deploy test contracts that haven't yet been fully debugged. You don't use real ETH to fuel transactions on testnets — you use the respective test ETH native to the testnet in question.

Testnets come in two flavors:

>> **Proof of work:** Only one testnet — the Ropsten Test Network — is based on a proof-of-work consensus protocol, making it the closest representation of the main Ethereum network.

We use the Ropsten Test Network in our step-by-step guide because it relies on proof of work, which, as we explain in Chapter 6, is the prevailing authority for Ethereum.

>> **Proof of authority:** The other testnets — Kovan, Rinkeby, and Görli/Goerli — are based on a proof-of-authority consensus protocol. With this protocol, a select group of nodes are authorized to validate transactions and add new blocks to the respective testnet blockchains.

Main network

The main Ethereum network, *Mainnet,* is where the real action — and anything of actual value — happens. Any Ethereum-based

NFT you've seen in the news or considered purchasing (such as *CryptoKitties* from Chapter 2) lives on the main Ethereum network.

REMEMBER

Whenever someone simply refers to Ethereum, they're referring to the main Ethereum network and not to the various testnets or private development environments.

Preparing Your Accounts (on MetaMask)

Begin by signing in to your MetaMask wallet. (For information about setting up MetaMask, see Chapter 2 and Chapter 4.) Your MetaMask wallet can hold numerous accounts, and you can create as many accounts as you want, as shown in Figure 7-7. Having separate accounts allows you to keep your Mainnet account (which contains real ETH) separate from your testnet and local accounts, where you can store test ETH and run practice transactions before trying them on Mainnet.

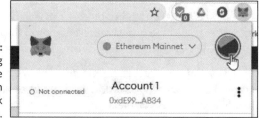

FIGURE 7-7:
Creating separate accounts in MetaMask app.

TIP

To create a new account, click the colorful circle in the upper-right corner of the MetaMask app (refer to Figure 7-7) and choose Create Account from the drop-down menu. Each separate account you create will have its own unique private key and public address. We recommend creating at least three separate accounts, with the following labels:

>> Mainnet Account

>> Testnet Account

>> Local Account

In later chapters, we show you how to set up your development environment (Chapter 8) and prepare to deploy your own smart contracts (Chapter 9). Trust us: When you reach that stage, you'll be glad you have separate accounts.

REMEMBER

We reference these account names as we continue our setup guide throughout this section, as well as when we continue the instructions for building your own non-fungible ERC-721 token in Chapters 8 through 11.

Renaming accounts on MetaMask

If you have already created accounts that you want to rename (which changes nothing else about the account), you can follow these steps:

1. Select the account you want to rename.

2. Click the vertical ellipsis to the right of the account name, as shown in Figure 7-8.

FIGURE 7-8: Navigating account options on MetaMask.

3. From the drop-down menu that appears, choose Account Details.

A new window is displayed with the account name above a QR code, as shown in Figure 7-9.

FIGURE 7-9:
Specific
account
details on
MetaMask.

4. Click the Pencil icon next to the account name.

5. Rename the account and then select the check box, to
the right of the text input box, to confirm the change,
as shown in Figure 7-10.

FIGURE 7-10:
Renaming an
account on
MetaMask.

Ta-da! The account now shows its new name.

REMEMBER

Changing account names on MetaMask doesn't alter the private key required in order to submit transactions or the public account address used to receive funds. These account names are purely a cosmetic feature to help you mentally organize different accounts for different uses.

Adding different ETH to different accounts

After you have your three accounts set up and named to help you keep things organized, you have to put some ETH into each one. This list highlights important differences to keep in mind while you fund each type of account:

>> *Mainnet account:* You want real ETH in this account so that you can fuel Ethereum transactions on Mainnet. (See Chapter 2 and Chapter 4 for details on how to fund your Mainnet account with actual ETH.)

>> *Local account:* Funding your local account is much simpler and cheaper because the test environment is locally confined to your personal system and because the ETH has no practical value outside of this local test environment. (You cannot spend this ETH outside of this local environment.)

When you initiate a private, practice blockchain, your local development environment also initiates local accounts prefunded with local test ETH. We explain how to import these local accounts, along with their test funds, into MetaMask in Chapter 8, where we show you how to set up your Ethereum stack.

>> *Testnet account:* To fuel your test transactions on the public testnets, you need network-specific test ETH. Here is where faucets come into play. A test ETH *faucet* provides test ETH at regular intervals, but you can request only so much test ETH in a given period. (For more on test faucets, check out the next section.)

Funding your testnet account

You can fund your testnet account with test ETH from various test networks. MetaMask helpfully provides a list — you choose which one you want and then go get your test ETH. We use the Ropsten Ethereum Faucet to fund our testnet account because we later use the Ropsten test network to practice deploying smart contracts.

To fund your testnet account, follow these steps:

1. **Go to the Ropsten Ethereum Faucet page at** https:// faucet.ropsten.be, **as shown in Figure 7-11.**

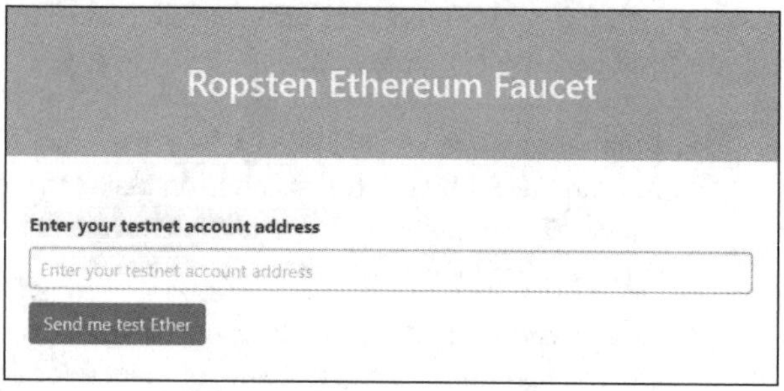

FIGURE 7-11:
The Ropsten
Ethereum
Faucet.

2. **Sign in to your MetaMask wallet.**

3. **Click the central dropdown menu to switch networks from the Ethereum Mainnet to the Ropsten test network, as shown in Figure 7-12.**

4. **Select your testnet account and click to copy the public account address, as shown in Figure 7-13.**

    In our example, this account address is 0x43371B75585785 D62e3a50533aa15ee8D350273F .

5. **Paste this account address into the Ropsten Ethereum Faucet and click the Send Me Test Ether button, as shown in Figure 7-14.**

6. **Wait approximately 1 minute.**

    Be patient — it might take a bit longer.

7. **Double-check that you now have a testnet account balance on MetaMask, as shown in Figure 7-15.**

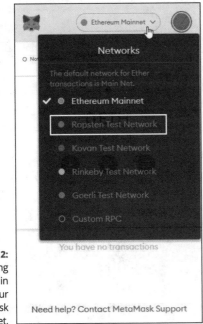

FIGURE 7-12:
Switching
networks in
your
MetaMask
wallet.

FIGURE 7-13:
Copying a
public
account
address
from your
MetaMask
wallet.

FIGURE 7-14:
Requesting
test ETH
from the
Ropsten
Ethereum
Faucet.

FIGURE 7-15:
Updated
testnet
account
balance,
after
requesting
test ETH.

Congratulations! You now have one test ETH in your testnet account.

REMEMBER

If you've waited longer than 10 minutes and still see no test ETH in your testnet account, make sure you've switched networks to the Ropsten test network, as outlined in Step 3 in the preceding step list.

WARNING

Testnet faucets don't provide an unlimited source of test ETH, and you will be greylisted if you request test ETH too soon after receiving what is affectionately known as "a drip." The Ropsten Ethereum Faucet even requires a 24-hour cooling-off period between requests. If you make another request before that period ends, you're *greylisted* and you have to wait an additional 24 hours before requesting more test ETH. (Figure 7-16 illustrates what such a reprimand looks like.)

FIGURE 7-16:
The greylist, warning when you request more test ETH too soon.

Exploring the Ropsten testnet blockchain

As with transactions on the Ethereum Mainnet, you can view your testnet transactions, along with all the other blocks of testnet transactions, on the Ropsten testnet blockchain. Here's how:

1. Go to https://ropsten.etherscan.io.

2. Type a specific transaction hash, block number, or account address to explore, as shown in Figure 7-17, and then click the Search button (the button with the Magnifying Glass icon).

Let's paste in the testnet account address from the previous example:

0x43371B75585785D62e3a50533aa15ee8D350273F

This search shows the transaction transferring a single test ETH into the testnet account we entered in Step 2, as shown in Figure 7-18.

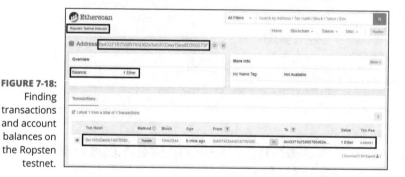

FIGURE 7-17:
Exploring
transactions
on the
Ropsten
testnet.

FIGURE 7-18:
Finding
transactions
and account
balances on
the Ropsten
testnet.

Of course, transactions and ETH associated with this testnet account aren't shuttled over to the Ethereum Mainnet, accessed at `https://etherscan.io`, as shown in Figure 7-19.

"Disappearing" balances

What if you suddenly see an account balance that's much different from what you think it should be? Don't panic. Instead, check to see which network you're on because MetaMask reflects your account balances within the selected network.

WARNING

If you switch the network on MetaMask from the Ropsten test network to the Ethereum Mainnet, as shown in Figure 7-20, the balance in your testnet account appropriately reflects 0 ETH (assuming you have no real ETH in this account).

FIGURE 7-19:
The Ethereum Mainnet doesn't reveal the test ETH balance.

FIGURE 7-20:
This testnet account contains 0 ETH when viewed on the Ethereum Mainnet.

Similarly, if you have real ETH in your Mainnet account, switching from the Ethereum Mainnet to the Ropsten test network suddenly reflects a balance of 0 ETH (assuming that you have no test ETH in that account).

Chapter **8**

Setting Up a Development Environment

I n this chapter, we introduce the elements of an Ethereum solution stack and walk you through the steps to set up your local development environment in Ganache. We also show you how to configure your MetaMask wallet to connect to your local test environment and import at least one of your local accounts. Finally, we cover synching the Remix-IDE to your MetaMask wallet.

TIP

Chapter 7 shows you the first critical step in the journey toward building your own non-fungible ERC-721 token (setting up your accounts), and this chapter covers the second critical step (setting up your development environment). We highly recommend that you read the full chapter in order to understand the basic features and selections we make along the way. If you're feeling antsy, though, you can skip straight to the last section "Put On Your Hard Hat: Constructing Your Environment."

To follow the step lists in this chapter, you need to have completed these steps in advance:

1. Install the MetaMask wallet (see Chapter 2 and Chapter 4).

2. Create at least three separate externally owned accounts (see Chapter 7):

   - *Mainnet*

   - *Testnet*

   - *Local*

Those accounts need funds — real ETH in your Mainnet account (see Chapter 2 and Chapter 4) and test ETH in your Testnet account (see Chapter 7).

Exploring Your Ethereum Solution Stack

A *solution stack* refers to a set of software components that creates a complete environment requiring no additional subsystems to support the development, deployment, and execution of your applications. You can custom build your own stack or choose premade stacks. We explain the necessary components of a full stack and walk you through building your own stack in this section.

Elements of the Ethereum stack

From a bird's-eye view, this list describes the typical elements of an Ethereum-based solution stack:

>> **The end-user application:** Of course, at the top of the stack is the end-user application itself!

CryptoKitties (www.cryptokitties.co) — introduced in Chapter 2 — is an example of an Ethereum-based end-user application.

>> **The Ethereum client API:** An application programming interface (API) is a bridge between applications, enabling them to communicate with each other. An Ethereum client API allows an end-user application to connect to Ethereum nodes so that the app can access information on the Ethereum blockchain (such as account balances, past transactions data, and smart contracts). The Ethereum client API also allows the application to submit transactions to the Ethereum network so that funds can be transferred, new smart contracts can be deployed, or code in existing smart contracts can be executed.

The API embedded by the MetaMask browser extension is an example of an Ethereum client API.

>> **The nodes and clients:** Ethereum *nodes* are computers acting as Ethereum *clients*, which means they run special client software that adheres to the rules governing the way . Ethereum validates, executes, and records transactions.

>> **The smart contracts:** Smart contracts contain the executable code that end-user applications rely on to perform various tasks. You can learn more about smart contracts, including how to deploy your own, in Chapter 9.

>> **The Ethereum Virtual Machine:** At the base of any Ethereum stack is the Ethereum Virtual Machine (EVM). The EVM, introduced in Chapter 6, embodies the distributed computing system of nodes that maintain updated copies of the Ethereum blockchain.

Across the layers of the Ethereum stack, these are the items that directly concern you in your quest to build your own non-fungible ERC-721 token:

>> The Ethereum client API

>> The elements required to develop, test, and deploy smart contracts — namely, a source code compiler and a testing environment

Here a stack, there a stack: Pre-made stacks

You have numerous development stacks to choose from — each differing in complexity and ambition — as shown on the menu of options at `https://ethereum.org/en/developers/local-environment`. (See Figure 8-1.)

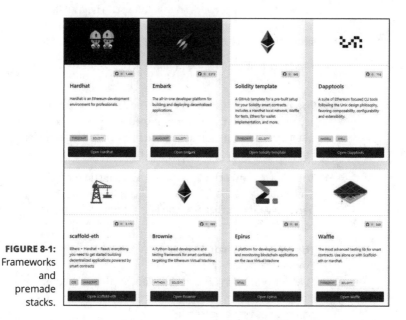

Unfortunately, no single package contains a ready-made, all-inclusive development stack. Thankfully, though, many blueprints are available to guide you through the components you need to install to complete the development environment that's right for your needs.

For this book, we have settled on the simplest combination of components that provide enough flexibility to customize features of your NFT but don't require working with command-line interfaces (CLIs), which is common among Ethereum core developers.

TECHNICAL STUFF

Graphical user interfaces (GUIs) provide a more user-friendly visual workspace that's easier to navigate than a CLI-based workspace, which has a text-based user interface that requires you to type commands.

Specifically, our step-by-step guide uses these elements:

>> MetaMask, for the Ethereum client API

>> Ganache GUI, for the local test blockchain

>> Remix IDE, for the source-code compiler

Put On Your Hard Hat: Constructing Your Environment

In this section, we explain how to implement a local blockchain on your personal computer. We then show you how to configure your MetaMask wallet for use with your local development environment as well as with the Remix IDE.

Setting up your local blockchain test environment

REMEMBER

As we explain in Chapter 7, a local development environment is a private and safe place for you to practice deploying and testing your smart contracts.

To set up your local development environment, follow the steps below to install the Ganache desktop application (Ganache GUI), which is part of Truffle Suite's toolkit of offerings for smart-contract developers.

1. Go to www.trufflesuite.com/ganache and **click the Download button, as shown in Figure 8-2, to download the Ganache desktop application.**

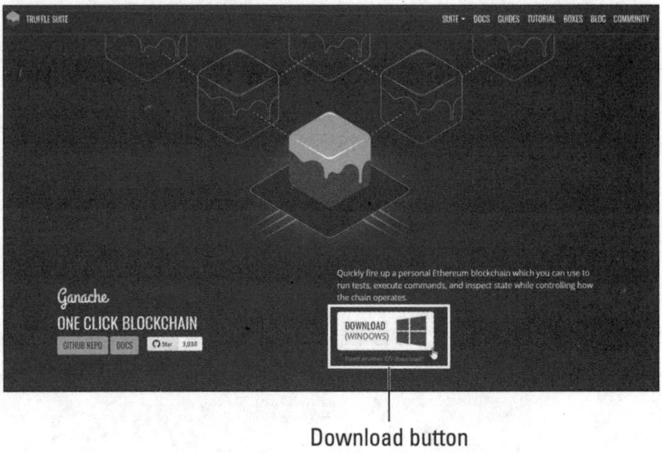

FIGURE 8-2:
Download
the
Ganache
desktop
application.

Download button

2. **When the download is complete, double-click the installa-tion package and follow the prompts to install Ganache, as shown in Figure 8-3.**

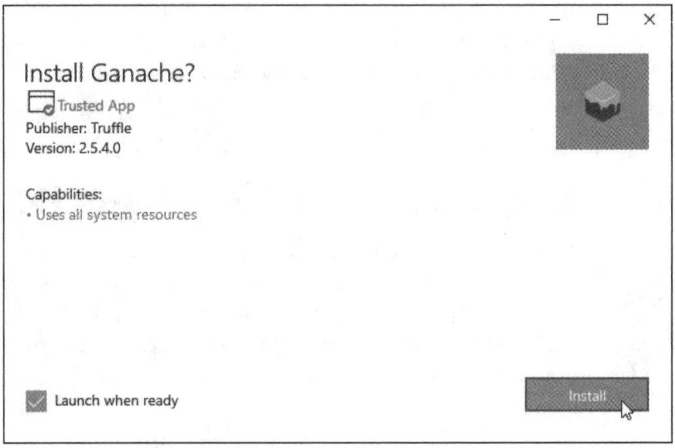

Install Ganache?

Trusted App

Publisher: Truffle
Version: 2.5.4.0

Capabilities:
• Uses all system resources

Launch when ready   Install

FIGURE 8-3:
The
Ganache
installer.

3. **When installation is complete, launch Ganache and then click the Quickstart Ethereum option on the start page, as shown in Figure 8-4.**

Ganache initiates a local blockchain with test accounts that mimic externally owned accounts on Ethereum, as shown in Figure 8-5.

Ganache's default setting is to initiate ten test accounts, each with a balance of 100 test ETH, which can be used only in this current workspace.

FIGURE 8-4:
The Ganache start screen.

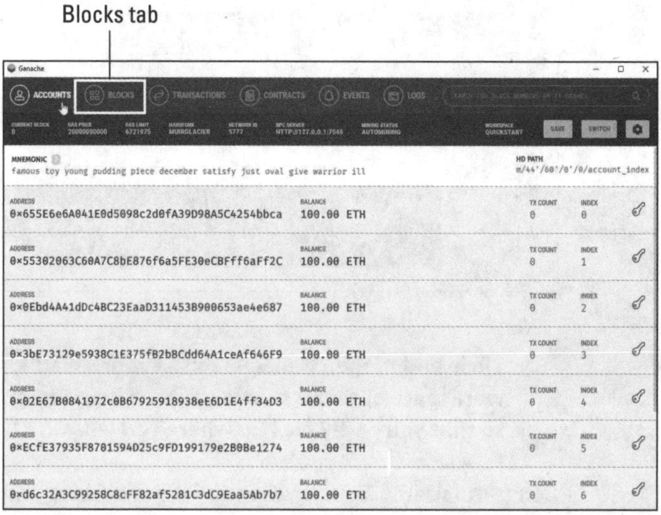

Blocks tab

FIGURE 8-5:
Ganache Accounts screen.

4. Click the Blocks tab (to the right of the Accounts tab on the menu running across the top of the screen) to see the entire blockchain ledger for your current workspace.

At initiation, you have just one block: Block 0 (the *genesis* block), as shown in Figure 8-6.

FIGURE 8-6:
The
Ganache
genesis
block at
initiation.

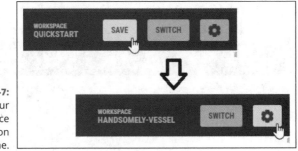

5. **Save your workspace by clicking the Save button in the upper-right corner of the Ganache application window. (Refer to Figure 8-6.)**

Ganache automatically (and randomly) names your workspace. In our case, Ganache has named our workspace Handsomely-Vessel. (See Figure 8-7.)

FIGURE 8-7:
Saving your
workspace
on
Ganache.

6. **Close and reopen Ganache to see your saved workspace(s) at the start page, as shown in Figure 8-8, so that you easily pick up where you left off.**

Congratulations! You're ready to begin working in your private development environment!

TIP

If you want to change the name of your workspace, click the Settings (Gear) icon to the right of your workspace name. (Refer to Figure 8-7.) A new screen appears, where you can edit your workspace name, as shown in Figure 8-9.

As for us, we're keeping the magnificent workspace name that Ganache has randomly generated for us: Handsomely-Vessel!

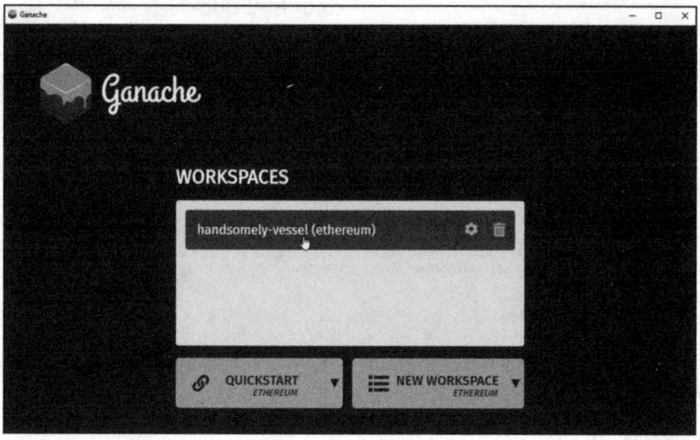

FIGURE 8-8:
The Ganache start page, after reinitiation.

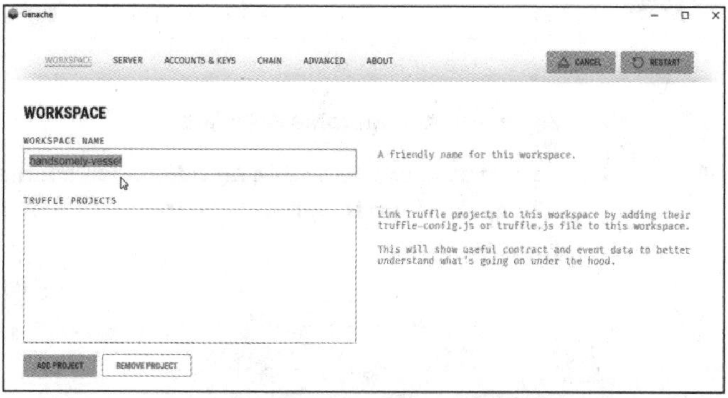

FIGURE 8-9:
Editing your workspace on Ganache.

Connecting a custom (Ganache) network to your MetaMask wallet

After you've fired up a local blockchain, you're ready to add this custom "network" and associated accounts to your MetaMask wallet. Follow these steps:

1. **Open Ganache and load the workspace you created in the preceding section.**

2. **Locate your RPC URL, which by default is http://127.0.0.1:7545, as shown in Figure 8-10.**

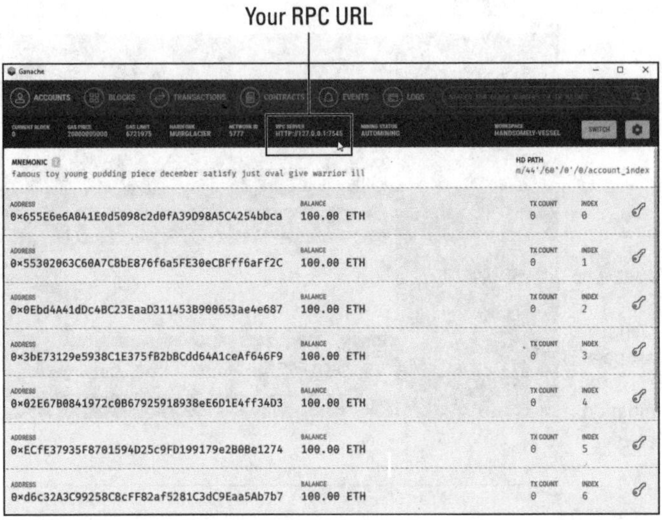

Your RPC URL

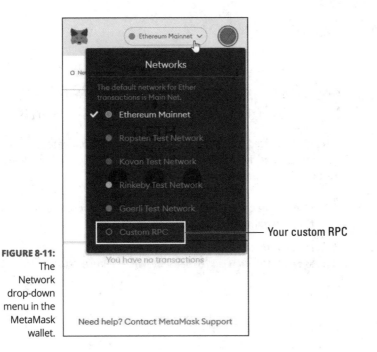

FIGURE 8-10:
Locating the
RPC URL
from the
Ganache
interface.

3. **Sign in to your MetaMask wallet.**

4. **To switch networks within MetaMask, select the Custom RPC option from the drop-down menu, as shown in Figure 8-11.**

Your custom RPC

FIGURE 8-11:
The
Network
drop-down
menu in the
MetaMask
wallet.

5. **On the new page that appears, shown in Figure 8-12, fill in the network name, the new RPC URL, and the chain ID, like this:**

- *Network name:* HANDSOMELY-VESSEL

  You can choose whatever network name you want. For consistency and to avoid confusion, we recommend using the name of the network you've chosen within your Ganache workspace.

- *New RPC URL:* http://127.0.0.1:7545 — the default RPC URL

- *Chain ID:* 1337 — the default Chain ID

6. **Click the Save button.**

Great work! You have successfully added a new network to your MetaMask network options, as shown in Figure 8-13.

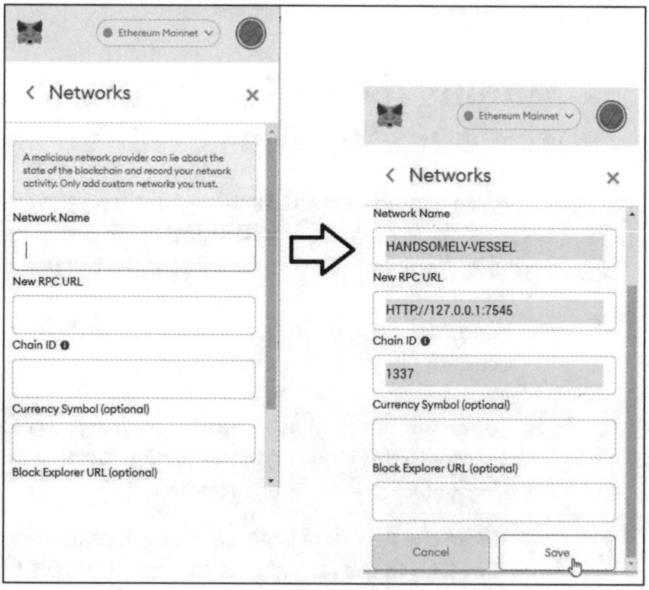

TIP

FIGURE 8-12:
Adding a
new
network to
MetaMask
wallet.

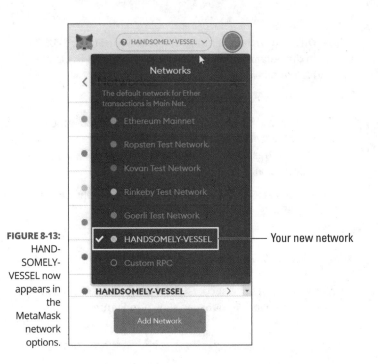

FIGURE 8-13:
HAND-
SOMELY-
VESSEL now
appears in
the
MetaMask
network
options.

Your new network

Adding local (Ganache) accounts to your MetaMask wallet

After you install Ganache and add the corresponding custom network in MetaMask, you'll want to import a couple of the accounts from your workspace in Ganache to MetaMask.

To import the local accounts, you need their private keys. To access the keys, follow these steps:

1. **Open Ganache and load the workspace you created earlier in this chapter, in the section "Setting up your local blockchain test environment."**

2. **From the Accounts page, select an account and click the Key icon to the far right, as shown in Figure 8-14.**

   The next pop-up screen provides the private key for this account, as shown in Figure 8-15.

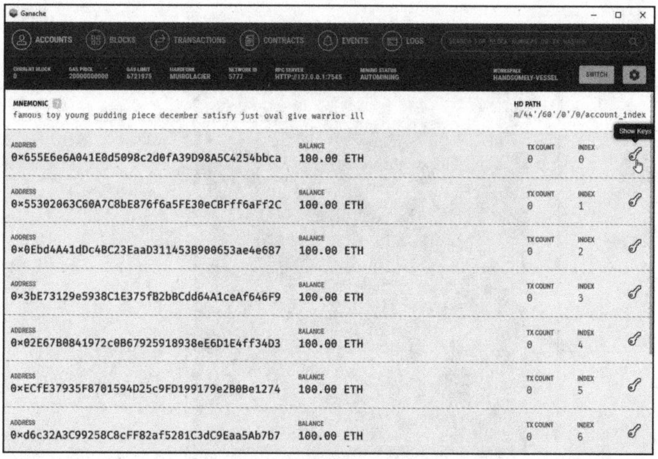

FIGURE 8-14:
Accessing
account
private keys
in your
Ganache
workspace.

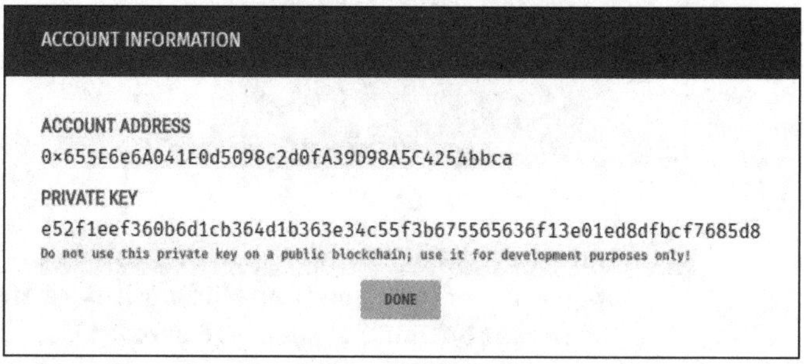

FIGURE 8-15:
Sample
account
address and
private key
in Ganache.

With the private key(s) in hand, here's how to import these
accounts into your MetaMask wallet:

1. **Sign in to your MetaMask wallet and switch to the
Handsomely-Vessel network.**

REMEMBER

Our custom network name is Handsomely-Vessel, which
may differ from the name of your custom network (from
the steps in the earlier section "Setting up your local
blockchain test environment section").

2. **Click the colorful circle in the upper-right corner of the
MetaMask app and select the Import Account option from
the drop-down menu, as shown in Figure 8-16.**

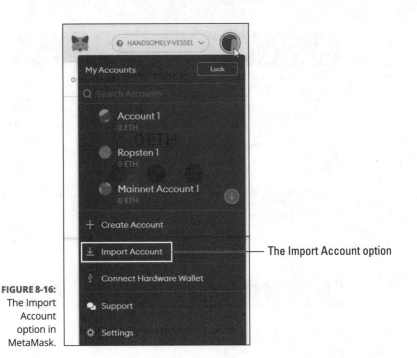

The Import Account option

FIGURE 8-16:
The Import
Account
option in
MetaMask.

3. **In the new dialog box that appears, paste in the private key of an account from your Ganache workspace and then click the Import button, as shown in Figure 8-17.**

Figure 8-18 shows the imported account in MetaMask. Note that we renamed the account.

TIP

Rename your imported account to make it easy to remember that it's a local Ganache account. We renamed our imported account "Ganache HV 1" because it relates to the original account name. To rename your accounts on MetaMask, click the vertical ellipsis to the right of the account name and select Account Details. Then click the Pencil icon next to the account name, rename the account, and click the check box to finalize the name change. (For more details, see Chapter 7.)

Ta-da! You have now successfully imported your local Ganache account into your MetaMask wallet.

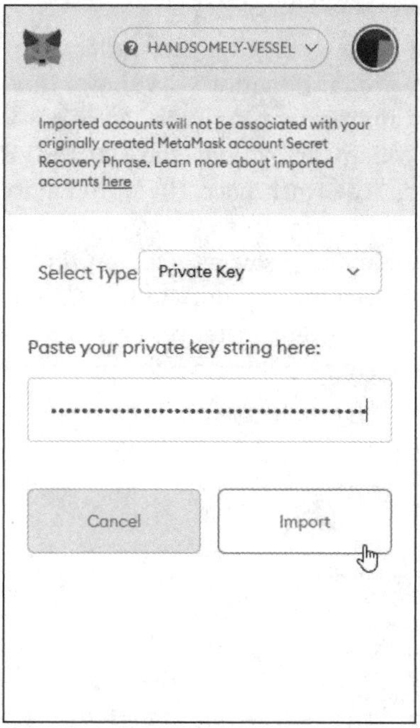

FIGURE 8-17:
Importing
an account
into your
MetaMask
wallet.

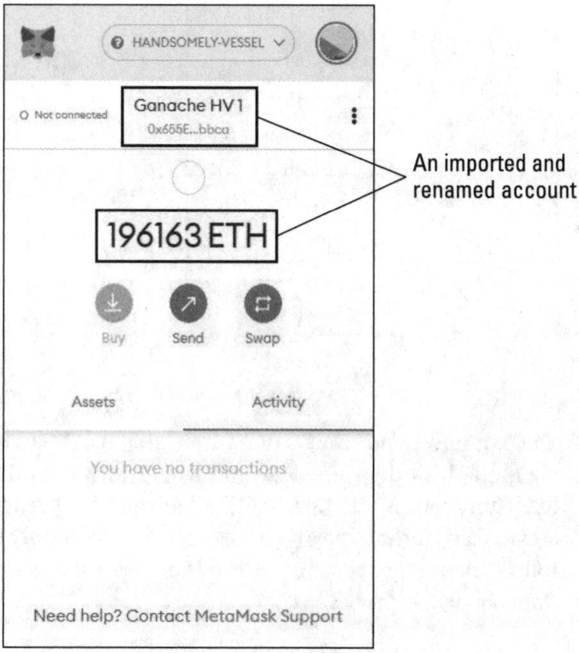

An imported and
renamed account

FIGURE 8-18:
A
successfully
imported
and
renamed
account in
MetaMask.

Don't panic if you see a strange balance reflected in your newly imported Ganache account. Figure 8-18 shows that, even when connected to the appropriate network, we have a balance of 196163 ETH (!), which far exceeds the 100 test ETH balance reflected in our Ganache workspace. (Refer to Figure 8-14.)

REMEMBER

As we explain in Chapter 7, you must be on the right network within MetaMask to see the appropriate test ETH or actual ETH in each of your accounts. For instance, Figure 8-19 shows that our Ganache HV 1 account reflects a balance of 0 ETH when we switch networks to the Ethereum Mainnet.

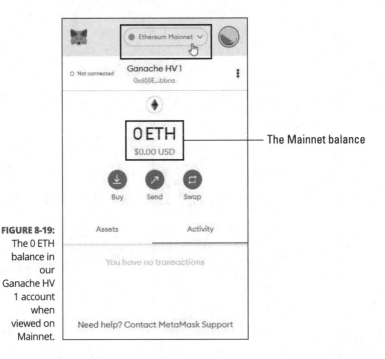

The Mainnet balance

FIGURE 8-19:
The 0 ETH
balance in
our
Ganache HV
1 account
when
viewed on
Mainnet.

You can now send transactions from this local Ganache account via MetaMask the same way you would with the other accounts loaded in your MetaMask wallet. You're not yet ready to submit a transaction that spawns a new contract account, but you can follow these steps to transfer funds across accounts in your local Ganache workspace:

1. On the Accounts tab, highlight a different account in your Ganache workspace and then right-click to copy the public account address, as shown in Figure 8-20.

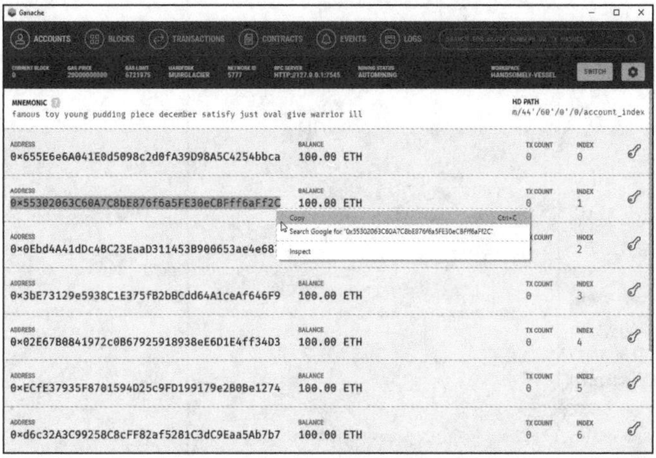

FIGURE 8-20:
Copying an account address in the Ganache workspace.

2. Follow the typical steps listed here for sending a transaction via MetaMask, as shown in Figure 8-21:

a. *Select the appropriate account:* In our case, it's our Ganache HV 1 account.

b. *Ensure that you're on the correct network:* We're on our Handsomely-Vessel custom network.

c. *Click the Send button.*

3. Paste in the address you copied from your Ganache workspace in Step 1 above, as shown in Figure 8-22, and then select how much to transfer. (We picked 5 test ETH.)

4. Click the Next button and then click the Confirm button on the page that follows.

The numbers you see at this stage may look strange, as we described in our earlier warning, due to unreconciled issues between MetaMask and the local Ganache environment.

REMEMBER

Because transactions and blocks are automatically mined on the local Ganache blockchain, the status of this submitted transaction quickly changes from *pending* to complete, as shown in Figure 8-23.

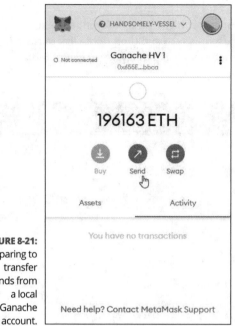

FIGURE 8-21:
Preparing to transfer funds from a local Ganache account.

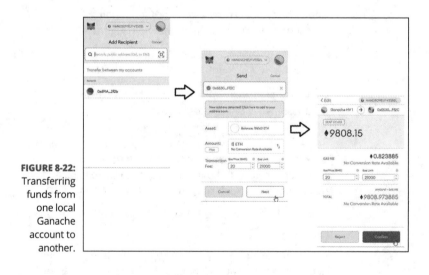

FIGURE 8-22:
Transferring funds from one local Ganache account to another.

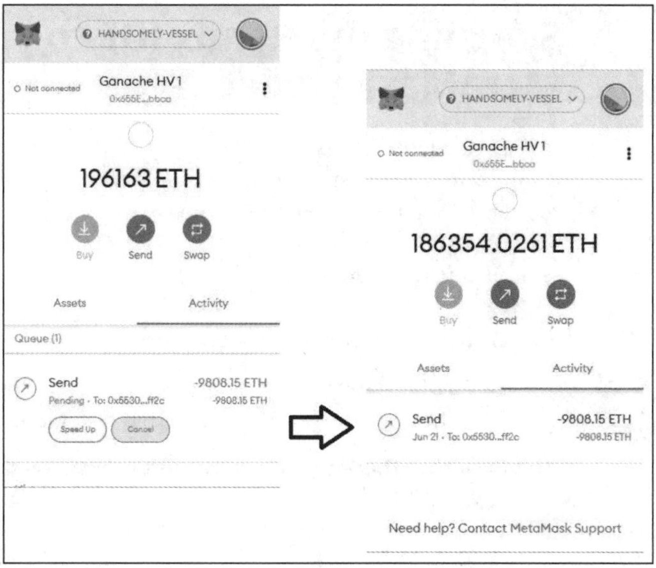

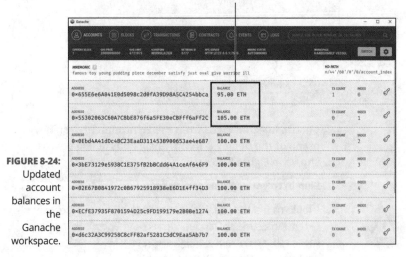

FIGURE 8-23:
Transaction
confirmation
in
MetaMask.

5. Check the account balances in your Ganache workspace.

Note that 5 test ETH has been moved from the first account to the second, as shown in Figure 8-24.

Your new balance

FIGURE 8-24:
Updated
account
balances in
the
Ganache
workspace.

Synching the Remix IDE to your MetaMask wallet

In this section, you explore Remix so that you can ultimately compile and deploy smart contracts — either in your local environment, on a testnet, or on Mainnet.

To find your way around Remix, follow these steps:

1. **Go to** http://remix.ethereum.org.

Be sure to type in http:// (without the *s*) and *not* https:// (with the *s*) or else Remix cannot access MetaMask.

2. **Click the Ethereum icon on the left toolbar, as shown in Figure 8-25.**

The Ethereum icon

FIGURE 8-25:
The Remix
main page.

3. **Choose Injected Web3 from the Environment drop-down menu of the Deploy & Run Transactions dialog box, as shown in Figure 8-26.**

4. **Sign in to your MetaMask wallet.**

Problems may arise if you've installed other wallet browser extensions, such as Dapper. We recommend disabling these other extensions and keeping only MetaMask as you continue our step-by-step guide.

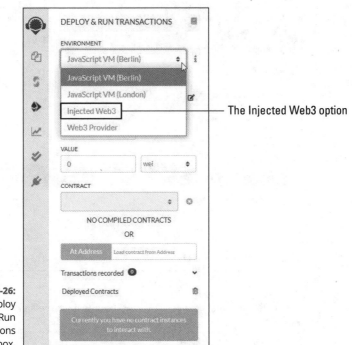

The Injected Web3 option

5. **(Optional) To turn off potentially problematic browser extensions, follow these steps:**

a. *Right-click the icon of the extension you want to disable from the browser toolbar.*

b. *Select Manage Extensions.*

c. *On the following page, use the toggle (see Figure 8-27) to turn off the browser extension in question.*

6. **Within MetaMask, select the network and account you want to work from.**

In Figure 8-28, we show our Remix environment when selecting the Ropsten test network along with the testnet account that we show you how to create and fund in Chapter 7.

Figure 8-29 shows our Remix environment when selecting our Handsomely-Vessel custom network along with the Ganache HV 1 account we imported and renamed earlier in this chapter.

Congratulations! You now have a fully functioning and self-contained solution stack to begin developing and deploying smart contracts.

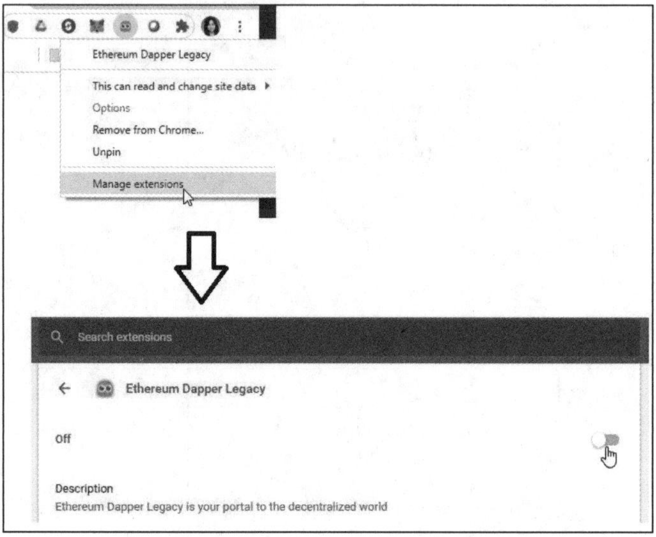

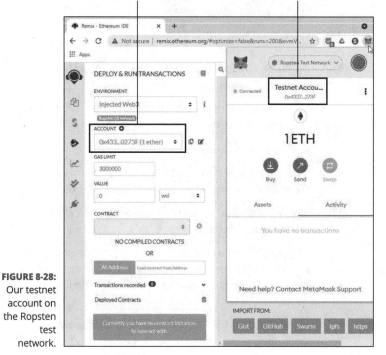

FIGURE 8-27:
Disabling
specific
browser
extensions.

The Ropsten test network   Your testnet account

FIGURE 8-28:
Our testnet
account on
the Ropsten
test
network.

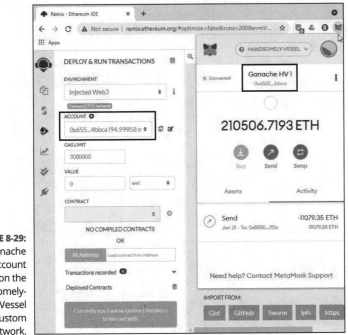

FIGURE 8-29: Our Ganache HV 1 account on the Handsomely-Vessel custom network.

Chapter **9**

Deploying Your First Smart Contract

This chapter walks you through the steps to develop, compile, and deploy your first smart contract. Before we get to those steps, though, we want to give you a quick introduction to smart contract languages and describe the elements of a smart contract. We also want to touch on smart contract libraries, which become more relevant in Chapter 10 and Chapter 11.

TIP

This chapter represents the final hands-on preparation you need before attempting to build your own non-fungible ERC-721 token. (See Chapter 11 for more on that topic.) We highly recommend reading the full chapter in order to more fully understand the basic features of smart contracts — as well as the reasoning behind the selections we make along the way. If you're feeling antsy, though, you can skip straight to the final section "Ready for Takeoff: Launching Your Smart Contract."

REMEMBER

To work through this chapter, you need to have first installed and set up a MetaMask wallet. (See Chapter 2 and Chapter 4.) You also need to have set up Mainnet, testnet, and local accounts, and you need to have set up a local Ganache environment and configured a corresponding custom network on MetaMask. (See Chapter 7 and Chapter 8.) Finally, you need to have set up the Remix-IDE browser (`http://remix.ethereum.org`) to synch to your Meta-Mask wallet. (Again, Chapter 8 can help you with that task.)

Working with Smart Contract Languages

To create a functional smart contract, you're essentially creating a contract account by submitting bytecode as a transaction (without a destination address) to the Ethereum network. Because *bytecode,* a machine-level code written in hexadecimal format, is difficult to learn and interpret, you need to use a supported and more human-like language — one that an existing compiler can translate into bytecode — to write your smart-contract source code.

Thankfully, you can choose from several actively maintained languages. Within the Remix IDE, which we've chosen for our step-by-step guide, the included compiler is designed to easily toggle between the Solidity and Yul languages:

>> **Solidity:** The Solidity programming language was specifically designed to implement smart contracts on the Ethereum Virtual Machine (EVM). It remains the primary language used by smart-contract developers on Ethereum, and its use has even spread to other competing platforms.

In the classification of programming languages, Solidity is considered a *high-level language:* It's easier to understand (by humans) and to debug, but it's less memory efficient and requires compilation to be translated into instructions that the executing machine can understand.

>> **Yul:** The newer programming language Yul requires greater mastery and understanding of *opcodes* (low-level, machine-language instructions) to use effectively. Yul is considered an intermediate, or mid-level, language.

After you select a language and write the source code for your contract, you then compile the code to produce these elements:

>> **Bytecode:** The bytecode consists of a set of instructions dictated entirely in a hexadecimal format that can be run on the EVM. Bytecode is a machine code, which, in the classification of programming languages, sits at the lowest level and is the most difficult for direct human interpretation.

>> **Opcode:** When you become better versed in the world of smart-contract development, you notice that many programmers reference commands from the opcode, which is an assembly language. The opcode instructions equate to what's conveyed by the bytecode but provide readable operation codes for what the processor should do. In the classification of programming languages, assembly language is considered a low-level language that sits just one layer above machine code.

>> **ABI:** The compiler also creates a corresponding application binary interface (ABI), which end-user applications need in order to navigate the contract's data and functions.

We're going with Solidity because it's the more commonly used language and the simplest one to work with. When you work with Solidity, you also have access to many more prebuilt libraries, which provided carefully developed and vetted code for you to build on. (We talk about prebuilt libraries in greater detail in the section "No Need to Reinvent the Wheel: Using Smart Contract Libraries," later in this chapter.)

Starting with the Solidity version pragma

To ensure that your Solidity source code isn't compiled under incompatible compiler versions, you should always include the

Solidity version pragma as the first line of your code. The *version pragma* specifies the allowable version(s) of the Solidity compiler to be used at compilation, as follows:

```
pragma solidity 0.8.6;
```

In this example, the version pragma allows our source code to be compiled only under version 0.8.6, ensuring that the code won't be compiled under a newer version that may have introduced updates that are incompatible with the code.

The version pragma syntax can be modified for greater flexibility. This list highlights a few examples:

>> <=0.8.6 allows compilers including and preceding version 0.8.6.

>> >=0.8.6 allows compilers including and following version 0.8.6.

>> ^0.8.6 allows compiler versions including and following version 0.8.6 but strictly preceding version 0.9.0 (the "^" specifies that compiler versions beyond 0.8.X should not be used).

In the version pragma syntax, the <= and >= modifiers can be used together to form allowances that are more customized than the narrowly specified ^ modifier. In addition, < and > are acceptable modifiers.

Going from source code to bytecode

Consider this simple smart-contract code written in Solidity:

```
pragma solidity 0.8.6;
contract LittleBear {
    string public msg = "Hello Little Bear (a.k.a.
    Maddie)!";
    }
```

When this particular Solidity source code is compiled, you end up with the following block of machine-level bytecode:

```
608060405234801561001057600080fd5b50600436106100
2b5760003560e01c80636b473fca14610030575b600080
fd5b61003861004e565b60405161004591906101155565b6
0405180910390f35b6000805461005b90610186565b8060
1f01602080910402602001604051908101604052809291
90818152602001828054610087906101865655b80156100d4
5780601f106100a9576101008083540402835291602001
9161001d4565b820191906000052602060002090 5b81548
15290600101906020018083116100b757829003601f168
201915b505050505081565b60006100e782610137565b6
100f1818561010142565b9350610101018156020860161015
3565b61010a816101e7565b84019150509029150505056 5b
60006020820190508181036000830152610121f81846100d
c565b905092915050565b600081519050919050565b6000
8282526020820190509291505056 5b60005b8 3811015 6
101715780820151818401526020810190506101015656
5b838111561018057600084840152b50505050565b
600060028204905060018216806101 9e57607f821
691505b6020821081141561019b2576101b16101b8
565b5b5091905056 5b7 f4e487b71000000000000000
00000000000000000000000000000000000000000000060
00526022600452600246000fd5b6000601 f19601 f8301
16905091905056fea264697066735822122067b6da
38f6dde0621c9c49d1785ec9d01d5d423d6d5f4aca
74e7b3f8ffa4c18f64736f6c63430008060033
```

A section of the corresponding opcode looks like this:

```
PUSH1 0x80 PUSH1 0x40 MSTORE CALLVALUE DUP1 ISZERO
PUSH2 0x10 JUMPI PUSH1 0x0 DUP1 REVERT JUMPDEST
POP PUSH1 0x4 CALLDATASIZE LT PUSH2 0x2B JUMPI
PUSH1 0x0 CALLDATALOAD PUSH1 0xE0 SHR DUP1 PUSH4
0x6B473FCA EQ PUSH2 0x30 JUMPI JUMPDEST PUSH1
0x0 DUP1 REVERT JUMPDEST PUSH2 0x38 PUSH2 0x4E
JUMP JUMPDEST PUSH1 0x40 MLOAD PUSH2 0x45 SWAP2
SWAP1 PUSH2 0x115 JUMP JUMPDEST PUSH1 0x40 MLOAD
DUP1 SWAP2 SUB SWAP1 RETURN JUMPDEST PUSH1 0x0
DUP1 SLOAD PUSH2 0x5B SWAP1 PUSH2 0x186 JUMP
JUMPDEST DUP1 PUSH1 0x1F ADD PUSH1  [...]
```

Finally, the following is the corresponding ABI that provides a roadmap for end user applications that want to interact with the this smart contract:

```
{
    "inputs": [],
    "name": "msg",
    "outputs": [
        {
                "internalType": "string",
                "name": "",
                "type": "string"
        }
    ],
    "stateMutability": "view",
    "type": "function"
}
```

You can probably see now why we prefer to write our smart-contract code in a high-level and more human-like language!

Key Elements of a Smart Contract

Smart contracts, at their core, consist of functions and data that are housed at the contract-account address on the Ethereum blockchain. In addition, when a transaction is executed to access functions in a smart contract, the state changes can be logged to the blockchain without being stored in the contract account, which is costlier. In this section, we unpack the meaning of these key elements of a smart contract — namely, its data, its functions, and its event logs.

Data

Solidity is a statically typed programming language, which means that the type (and, usually, size) of a variable must be specified in the source code before compilation.

Variables can be placed in storage as part of the contract data; these variables are defined as *state variables*. On the other hand, you may also have fleeting variables, used only for interim computations, that do not need to be retained from iteration to iteration; these variables are known as *memory variables*.

The information stored in state variables can also be accessed by other smart contracts if they're declared as *public* state variables. Otherwise, the information is considered *private* and is accessible only within the smart contract in which it is stored (though it can still be viewed by anyone because private state variables are stored on the public blockchain).

REMEMBER

Whether the stored data is public or private, only the contract in which the data is stored can alter the value of its state variables.

Functions

Smart-contract functions are where the action is. For instance, functions can be used to perform calculations, set new values for state variables, retrieve data from elsewhere on the blockchain, send ETH to other addresses, or call other functions. Functions fall into these three broad categories:

>> **Built-in functions:** Solidity has a menu of built-in functions that perform common tasks, such as `receive()` to receive ETH and `address.send()` to send ETH to a specified address. Another popular built-in function is `selfdestruct(address)`, which sends any remaining ETH in the contract account to the specified address then deletes the contract.

>> **Constructor functions:** Each contract can specify a `constructor()` function, which is executed only once when the smart contract is first deployed on the EVM.

>> **Custom functions:** And, of course, you can write your own functions!

When writing your own functions, you need to declare each function's accessibility by other functions, contracts, or transactions using the following keywords:

>> **Public/External:**

Public functions, which are the default, provide the most flexibility. They can be called by other functions within the contract, by other contracts, and by transactions submitted from externally owned accounts.

External functions provide the same degree of accessibility as public functions except that function calls within the contract are treated as though they are external calls and must be accompanied by the keyword this as a prefix.

>> **Private/Internal:**

Private functions can be called only from within the contract in which they're housed.

Solidity also has a feature that allows programmers to combine contracts into a new *derived contract,* one that inherits code from another contract. The contract being fed into the derived contract is the *base contract. Internal* functions are like private functions, except that they can also be called by their derived contracts.

Event logs

Event logs provide a convenient way for you to store historical instances of information on the blockchain without declaring additional storage space in your contract account. Other smart contracts (or people) can view these logs for an account of changes that have occurred. Events can be declared in a contract using the keyword event. When called (using the keyword emit), the arguments are stored on the blockchain in a log associated with the contract address.

The sample smart contract that you deploy later in this chapter, in the section "Ready for Takeoff: Launching Your Smart Contract," provides an example of how an event is declared and emitted.

No Need to Reinvent the Wheel: Using Smart Contract Libraries

A plethora of smart-contract libraries are available to provide you prebuilt functions and implementations of Ethereum development standards. (For more on this topic, see Chapter 10.) In addition to saving you the foundational work, predeveloped and prevetted open source libraries provide added security for less-expert developers who aren't intimately familiar with the finer considerations when it comes to smart-contract development and operations.

REMEMBER

The smart contract we show you how to deploy in the following section is simple enough that you needn't worry about using smart-contract libraries quite yet. In Chapter 11, where we show you how to build your own ERC-721 Token, you can learn how to load prebuilt libraries and import your desired base contracts.

Ready for Takeoff: Launching Your Smart Contract

The following steps walk you through deploying your first smart contract onto the EVM (or the Ropsten Testnet, if you're not ready to spend any real ETH yet):

1. **Go to** `http://remix.ethereum.org`.

   REMEMBER

   You must type `http://` (without the *s*) and *not* `https://` (with the *s*) or else Remix cannot access MetaMask.

2. **Click the New File link under the File heading on the main page, as shown in Figure 9-1.**

   A new file opens in the File Explorers pane, located on the left side of the page.

   At any time, the Double Page icon, located on the navigation pane on the far left, brings you back to the File Explorers pane, as shown in Figure 9-2.

   TIP

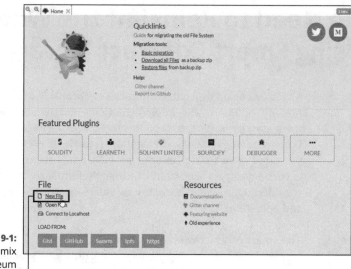

FIGURE 9-1:
The Remix
Ethereum
main page. New file

Click here to return to the File Explorers view.

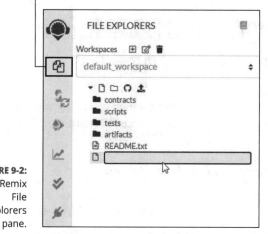

FIGURE 9-2:
The Remix
File
Explorers
pane.

3. **Using the cursor, click into the blank text box, type LittleBear.sol, and then press Enter.**

   A new tab pops up with the name of the file, as shown in Figure 9-3.

Excellent. You're now ready to enter your Solidity code!

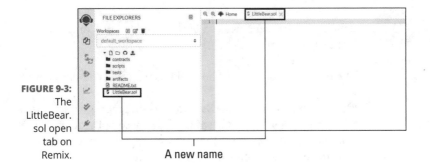

FIGURE 9-3:
The LittleBear.sol open tab on Remix.

A new name

Beginning with a simple template

Enter the following code into the LittleBear.sol file:

```solidity
pragma solidity 0.8.6;

contract LittleBear {

    event LogMsg(string message);

    string public storedMsg;

    constructor() {
    storedMsg = "Hello Little Bear (a.k.a.
        Maddie)!";
    emit LogMsg(storedMsg);
    }

    function updateMsg(string memory newMsg)
        public {
    storedMsg = newMsg;
    emit LogMsg(storedMsg);
    }

}
```

TIP

To avoid typos, you can copy-and-paste this snippet directly from www.seoyoungkim.com/nftfdcode.html.

Solidity is case sensitive, so LogMsg and logmsg aren't treated identically at compilation.

The remainder of this section explains the code, chunk by chunk.

This first line of code is the Solidity version pragma, which specifies the allowable version(s) of the Solidity compiler to be used at compilation. In this case, the version pragma allows the source code to be compiled only under version 0.8.6:

```
pragma solidity 0.8.6;
```

Next, you define the contract, LittleBear — Solidity is a *curly-bracket* language, which means it uses curly brackets to open and close blocks of code:

```
contract LittleBear {
```

The following line declares an event, LogMsg, that accepts a single argument of type string:

```
event LogMsg(string message);
```

The next line declares a public state variable, storedMsg, of type string. The latest content of storedMsg is retained in contract storage, even as the contract and its functions lie dormant between calls:

```
string public storedMsg;
```

The following block of code declares the special constructor() function, which is executed just once, at contract initiation. The first line of this function initializes the text being stored in the storedMsg state variable; the second line triggers the LogMsg event, passing the contents of storedMsg to be written to the contract's event log:

```
constructor() {
    storedMsg = "Hello Little Bear (a.k.a.
  Maddie)!";
    emit LogMsg(storedMsg);
}
```

The following block of code declares a public function, updateMsg( ), that accepts a single argument of type string. This parameter is defined by the name newMsg within this function and is declared as a memory variable, which means its contents aren't retained after the iteration of this function is complete. Without explicitly declaring the keyword memory, function parameters are, by default, memory variables as opposed to state variables:

```
function updateMsg(string memory newMsg) public {
    storedMsg = newMsg;
    emit LogMsg(storedMsg);
}
```

The first line of this updateMsg( ) function replaces the text being stored in the storedMsg state variable with the text that was passed to this function when it was called. The second line triggers the LogMsg event so that the latest contents of storedMsg can be written to the contract's event log.

Finally, we complete the block of contract code with a closing curly bracket:

```
}
```

Compiling before takeoff

After you prepare your LittleBear.sol file and add the necessary code, you can compile that code by following these steps:

1. **Click the Compiler icon located in the navigation pane on the left, as shown in Figure 9-4.**

2. **In the Solidity Compiler pane that appears, click the Compile LittleBear.sol button, as shown in Figure 9-5.**

    The compilation details for this contract appear underneath the Compile button, as shown in Figure 9-6.

Excellent! You're now ready to deploy your smart contract.

REMEMBER

After you deploy your smart contract, you can't go back and change any of the code. If you want to make corrections, you have to deploy a new smart contract with the updated code.

Compile icon

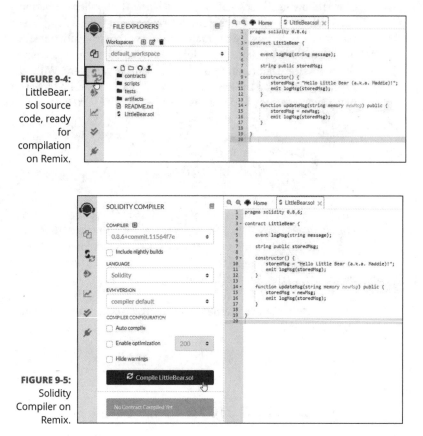

FIGURE 9-4:
LittleBear.
sol source
code, ready
for
compilation
on Remix.

FIGURE 9-5:
Solidity
Compiler on
Remix.

Deploying

Before you get to the real thing, practice deploying this contract on your local Ganache environment (which we discuss in Chapter 8).

1. **Click the Ethereum icon in the navigation pane on the left (the icon beneath the Compiler icon).**

This step opens the Deploy & Run Transactions pane, shown in Figure 9-7.

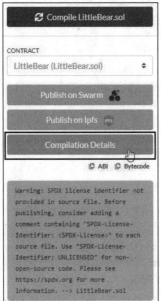

FIGURE 9-6:
Accessing compilation details on Remix.

The Ethereum icon

FIGURE 9-7:
Deploy & Run Transactions on Remix.

2. Select the Injected Web3 option from the Environment drop-down menu.

Make sure to also

a. Sign in to the MetaMask browser extension by clicking the Fox icon on the browser toolbar. (See Figure 9-8.)

b. Connect to the Handsomely-Vessel custom network.

c. Select one of your imported local Ganache accounts. In our case, we're choosing Ganache HV1.

You must also have the Ganache desktop application open and running the appropriate workspace — in this case, the Handsomely-Vessel workspace.

REMEMBER

3. Select the LittleBear–LittleBear.sol contract from the Contract drop-down menu and then click the Deploy button. (See Figure 9-8.)

Choose an account.   Choose a custom network.

Choose an environment.   Sign in to the MetaMask browser.

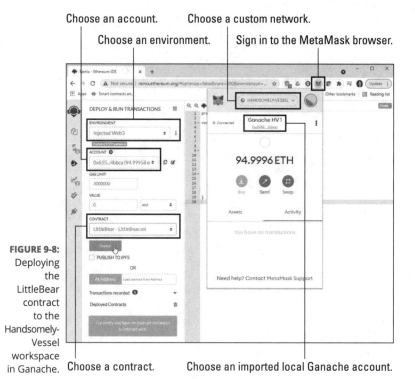

FIGURE 9-8: Deploying the LittleBear contract to the Handsomely-Vessel workspace in Ganache.

Choose a contract.   Choose an imported local Ganache account.

4. In the MetaMask notification pop-up that appears (see Figure 9-9), review the transaction details and click Confirm.

Clicking Confirm submits a transaction containing the compiled bytecode (without specifying a destination address), which generates a contract account with its own address for future access. If you realize that you're not ready to deploy your contract, simply click Reject.

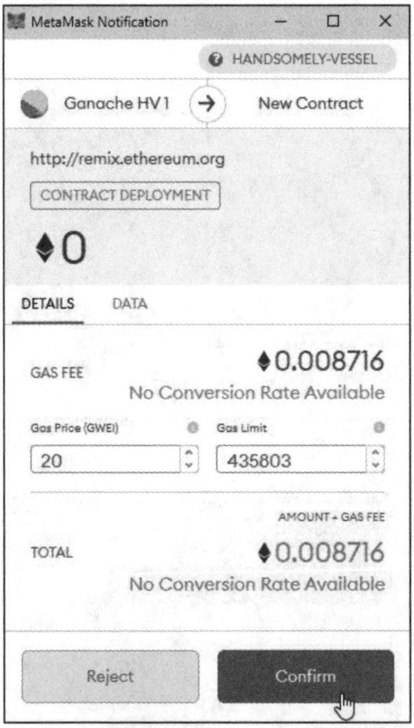

FIGURE 9-9: Confirming contract account creation on the Handsomely-Vessel workspace.

You can now view and interact with this contract under the Deployed Contracts heading, as shown in Figure 9-10:

- Click the storedMsg button to see what's currently stored in this state variable.

- Click the updateMsg button to call the function that updates the stored text in storedMsg, as shown in Figure 9-11.

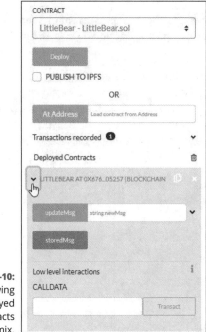

FIGURE 9-10:
Viewing deployed contracts on Remix.

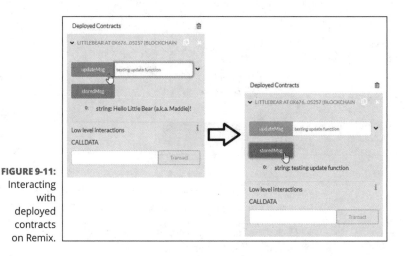

FIGURE 9-11:
Interacting with deployed contracts on Remix.

REMEMBER

Executing the updateMsg function is a transaction on the EVM that requires gas, whereas simply viewing the contents of the storedMsg variable doesn't require gas. You notice a MetaMask notification pop-up, requiring confirmation every time you attempt to execute the updateMsg function.

Now that you've gotten your feet wet in the local Ganache environment, it's time to deploy our `LittleBear` contract to the Ropsten Testnet. Follow these steps:

1. **Click the Fox icon in your browser toolbar to open MetaMask.**

2. **Switch networks to the Ropsten test network and then select your Testnet account (which you can see how to create and fund with Ropsten Test ETH in Chapter 7).**

   The account information on Remix's Deploy & Run Transactions pane changes accordingly, as shown in Figure 9-12.

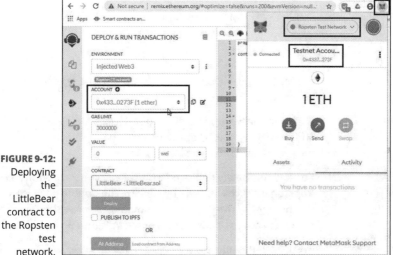

FIGURE 9-12: Deploying the LittleBear contract to the Ropsten test network.

3. **Click the Deploy button and confirm the transaction in the MetaMask notification that pops up, as shown in Figure 9-13.**

REMEMBER

   The transaction takes longer to mine this time because blocks on the Ropsten test network aren't automatically mined, as they are on local blockchain instances in the Ganache environment.

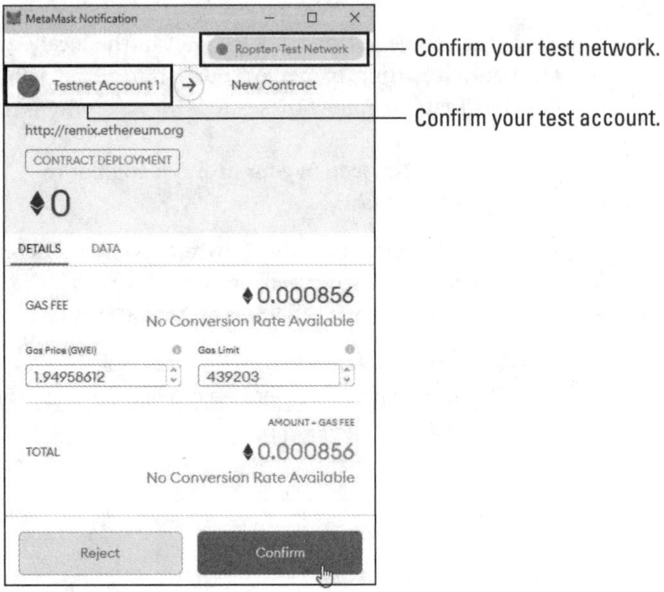

FIGURE 9-13:
Confirming
contract
account
creation on
the Ropsten
test
network.

4. **Access the** updateMsg **function to update the text that's being stored.**

We're making two updates: first to say, "Hello Mama Kim!" and next to say, "Hello Papa Kim!" Both changes appear in the event logs shown a bit later, in Figure 9-17.

5. **To view this newly deployed** LittleBear **contract on the Ropsten blockchain, start by clicking the double-page icon (to the right of the** LittleBear **heading) to copy the contract account address, as shown in Figure 9-14.**

In our case, this address is 0x1F922670Ce8bC699e780b9b 12960Fb80F998573e

6. **Point your browser to** https://ropsten.etherscan.io, **paste the contract account address into the search bar, as shown in Figure 9-15, and then click the Search button.**

Figure 9-16 shows that our contract has three transactions associated with it: the transaction that created the contract followed by two transactions to call the updateMsg function. Note that the newest transactions appear on top.

7. Click the Events tab to view the event logs created by
our contract. *Hint:* For the sake of readability, use the
drop-down tabs to convert the log outputs from Hex to
Text, **as shown in Figure 9-17.**

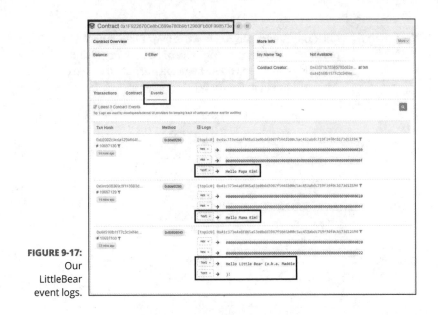

FIGURE 9-17:
Our
LittleBear
event logs.

Ta-da! You have now successfully deployed your first smart contract onto a public blockchain. At this point, you can repeat the preceding steps to deploy this contract on the Ethereum Mainnet. As for us, we're opting to save our valuable (real!) ETH and to avoid adding unnecessary baggage to the EVM because we don't plan to use our LittleBear contract other than to demonstrate how to deploy a smart contract.

IN THIS CHAPTER

» **Getting to know Ethereum development standards**

» **Looking at token interfaces**

» **Exploring ERC-20 (fungible) tokens**

» **Diving into ERC-721 non-fungible tokens**

Chapter **10**

Discovering Token Standards

This chapter takes a break from hands-on implementation to introduce Ethereum development standards as well as two widely used token standards: ERC-20 and ERC-721. As usual, we highly recommend reading the full chapter to immerse yourself in token lingo and to develop a greater appreciation of the instructions in our practical implementation.

That said, the knowledge contained in this chapter isn't required in order to continue creating your own NFT. So, if you're feeling antsy, you can skip straight to Chapter 11.

Introducing Ethereum Development Standards

Given the complex interdependency across the contracts, clients, and wallet services that make up the Ethereum ecosystem, the Ethereum community has a procedure in place to propose and establish development standards to follow when writing smart contracts for common use cases. You aren't required to adhere to these standards when developing your own tokens or dApps, but following established guidelines certainly makes your life easier.

Ensuring interoperability and composability

So how does standardization impact development?

First, standardization ensures interoperability. Ethereum clients and wallets are programmed to execute contract calls or to accept tokens, and adhering to accepted development standards ensures that this decentralized nexus of players remain compatible. You can liken this to the standardization in the size and shape of credit cards across various issuers, which ensures readability across various credit card processors and conformity across credit card slots in wallets.

Second, standardization promotes *composability*, which refers to the system's ability to allow developers to mix and match combinations of existing contracts to compose a functional customized solution. For example, think of LEGO bricks: The standardization of the studs and antistuds across bricks allows you to build many different and creative products. Yes, the world of LEGO has designed a highly composable system!

Learning the ABCs of EIPs and ERCs

To explain the commonly seen terms ERC-20 and ERC-721, we begin by defining and describing an Ethereum Improvement Proposal (EIP), since an Ethereum Request for Comment (ERC) is a special type of EIP.

A developer who wants to put forward a new development standard must first submit an EIP draft for consideration by the Ethereum community of core developers. In fact, the first EIP, numbered EIP-1, outlines the purpose of EIPs, guidelines for what an EIP should include, and the workflow process outlining the path from ideation to finalization or withdrawal. (See

Figure 10-1.) This process is based on processes adopted by the Python and Bitcoin communities, who established Python Enhancement Proposals (PEPs) and Bitcoin Improvement Proposals (BIPs), respectively.

FIGURE 10-1:
The EIP
workflow
diagram
from EIP-1.

Accessed at https://eips.ethereum.org/EIPS/eip-1.

Each new EIP not only improves the system but also enhances the development community's understanding of the strengths and weaknesses of the Ethereum Virtual Machine (EVM). EIPs can also foster creative thinking regarding additional use cases for the Ethereum platform.

The following list describes the three types of EIPs and gives examples of each:

>> **Standards Track EIPs** set forth changes to standards that impact most, if not all, activity on the Ethereum network. The Standards Track category has the following four important subclassifications, which range in the degree of system-wide impact and ramifications for interoperability:

- *Core EIPs* pertain to the consensus layer, which specifies the rules by which transactions settle and, ultimately, how the network agrees on a particular state and history of the EVM.

  Examples include EIP-2929, which increased the gas required for execution of certain opcodes, and the most recently finalized Core EIP-3554, which slowed the exponentially increasing block-difficulty level (a feature known as the *difficulty bomb*).

Opcodes, which we introduce in Chapter 9, are machine-language instructions providing readable operation codes to be processed.

- *Networking EIPs* pertain to the networking layer, which specifies how information is exchanged and propagated across nodes on the Ethereum network.

  For instance, the most recently finalized Networking EIP-2124, titled "Fork identifier for chain compatibility checks," provides a recordkeeping and validation mechanism to efficiently identify compatible peer nodes.

- *Interface EIPs* pertain to the application programming interface (API) / remote procedure call (RPC) layer, which specifies the connection between applications and how applications are executed across a distributed network. Interface EIPs also pertain to language-level standards — the ones which govern method names in code and how computations are submitted to the operating system.

  Examples include EIP-6, which introduced the SELFDESTRUCT opcode in lieu of the SUICIDE opcode to acknowledge the realities of mental health issues, and EIP-1193, which introduced a standardized format for JavaScript APIs to ensure compatibility across Ethereum wallet services and web applications.

- *Ethereum Request for Comment (ERC) EIPs* pertain to the applications layer, which specifies standards to ensure that different applications across the Ethereum ecosystem can seamlessly interact and share information. For instance, these standards ensure compatibility between tokens and wallet services and enhance composability by proposing conventions for smart-contract libraries and packages.

  Examples include the famous EIP-20 (ERC-20), which introduced the standards for implementing a fungible token, and EIP-721 (ERC-271), which introduced the standards for implementing a non-fungible token.

>> **Meta EIPs** summarize major changes to Ethereum and set forth procedures for the Ethereum community to propose changes to existing processes. EIP-1 is an example of a Meta EIP. EIP-4, which delineates Standards Track EIPs into finer subcategories, is another example of a Meta EIP. Other examples of Meta EIPs include a series of Hardfork Metas, which summarize major updates to the consensus layer.

>> **Informational EIPs** provide general information or suggestive guidelines to the Ethereum community.

For instance, EIP-2228, titled "Canonicalize the name of network ID 1 and chain ID 1," suggests that references to the main Ethereum network be standardized as proper nouns: Ethereum Mainnet or simply Mainnet.

With the basic idea behind EIPs in mind, you can take a deeper dive into the specific ERCs that provide the prevailing standards for token issuance on Ethereum.

Understanding Standard Token Interfaces

Token interfaces provide an outline declaring the functions and events to be implemented in a particular token contract. Adopting a standard interface enables tokens to easily conform to wallet services and exchanges that are, in turn, programmed to interact with tokens implementing that particular interface. Interfaces are declared in Solidity (a programming language we introduce in Chapter 9) as follows:

```
interface InterfaceName { }
```

An interface looks much like the skeleton outline of a contract, where functions and events are declared but are not implemented.

EIP-20, which was created on November 19, 2015, provided the first widely used token standard on Ethereum: the ERC-20 token. This proposal provided a standard interface for fungible tokens on Ethereum, and additional standards followed to enhance the functionality of this fungible-token standard.

Many notable cryptocurrencies, such as Tether (USDT) and Chainlink (LINK), were minted based on this standard and continue to trade as ERC-20 (or enhanced) tokens on the Ethereum blockchain. Others, such as EOS and Binance Coin (BNB), began as ERC-20 tokens before being swapped for their respective projects' native tokens after the separate blockchain platforms had been built. As of August 2021, Ethereum had more than 445,000 ERC-20 token contracts outstanding.

Inspired by the ERC-20 token standard, EIP-721 was created to provide a standard interface for non-fungible tokens on Ethereum. (Yes, we're talking NFTs!) The ERC-20 token standard treats its tokens as identical (and therefore fungible). The ERC-721 non-fungible token standard treats each token as a unique asset, each with its own distinguishable tokenID. Thus, digital collectibles such as *CryptoKitties* and Art Blocks were born! As of August 2021, Ethereum had close to 15,000 ERC-721 token contracts outstanding.

The following sections look at the interfaces for each of these token standards in greater detail.

ERC-20 token standard

To be ERC-20 compliant, a token contract must implement a number of elements contained within the ERC-20 standard interface. All functions and events must be declared with the same naming conventions dictated by the interface.

Let's begin by looking at the required functions:

> `totalSupply()`, `name()`, `symbol()`, and `decimals()`: These functions return the values stored in their respective namesake state variables. (the `name()`, `symbol()`, and `decimals()` functions are optional in this interface).
>
> `balanceOf(address _owner)`: This function returns the balance of the account with address `_owner`.

`transfer(address _to, uint256 _value)`: This function transfers _value tokens from the caller's account to the account with address _to.

`transferFrom(address _from, address _to, uint256 _value)`: This function transfers _value tokens from one specified account (_from) to another (_to).

`approve(address _spender, uint256 _value)`: This function permits the specified account (_spender) to withdraw up to _value tokens from the caller's account.

`allowance(address _owner, address _spender)`: This function returns the amount that account _spender is currently allowed to withdraw from account _owner.

Now let's look at the events declared in the ERC-20 interface:

`Transfer(address indexed _from, address indexed _to, uint256 _value)`: This event must be emitted when tokens are transferred from one account to another.

`Approval(address indexed _owner, address indexed _spender, uint256 _value)`: This event must be emitted each time an account approves an amount to be withdrawn by another account.

In implementing the ERC-20 interface, some state variables must also be stored in the token contract. Although the names of the required functions and events must be preserved as dictated by the interface, the following state variables can be declared and defined however you see fit in your particular implementation of the interface.

» `balances[]`: This variable stores the token balances of each account. (Note that this variable is an array.)

» `allowances[][]`: This variable stores the amounts that one account is currently allowed to withdraw from the other. (Note that this variable is a matrix.)

» `totalSupply`: This variable stores the total token supply.

» name (*optional*): This variable stores the name of the token (such as Tether).

>> `symbol` (*optional*): This variable stores the symbol of the token (such as USDT, in the case of Tether).

>> `decimals` (optional): This variable stores the number of decimals the token uses (that is, the token's divisibility).

TECHNICAL STUFF

Different implementations may require additional functions or variables, but you must, at a minimum, name and implement the functions and events declared in the ERC-20 interface as specified by the interface. The variable names declared in your implementation of the ERC-20 interface do not impact the interoperability of your token contract with any other contract that's expecting to interact with an ERC-20 token.

ERC-721 non-fungible token standard

To be ERC-721 compliant, a token contract must implement the following elements of the ERC-721 interface and ERC-165 interface. All functions and events must be declared with the same naming conventions dictated by these interfaces.

Let's begin by looking at the required functions:

`name()` and `symbol()`: These optional functions return the values stored in their respective namesake state variable.

`balanceOf(address _owner)`: This function returns the number of NFTs in the account with address `_owner`.

`ownerOf(uint256 _tokenId)`: This function returns the address of the account that owns the specified NFT, `_tokenId`.

`safeTransferFrom(address _from, address _to, uint256 _tokenId, bytes data)`: This function transfers the specified NFT, `_tokenId`, from one specified account (`_from`) to another (`_to`) and also passes data to the recipient account (`_to`).

`safeTransferFrom(address _from, address _to, uint256 _tokenId)`: This function transfers the specified NFT, `_tokenId`, from one specified account (`_from`) to another (`_to`).

`transferFrom(address _from, address _to, uint256 _tokenId)`: This function is similar to `safeTransferFrom` but doesn't verify whether the recipient account (_to) can receive NFTs.

`approve(address _approved, uint256 _tokenId)`: This function permits the specified account (_approved) to transfer the specified NFT (_tokenID).

`setApprovalForAll(address _operator, bool _approved)`: This function toggles the permission setting for whether the specified account (_operator) has transfer rights for all NFTs in your account.

`getApproved(uint256 _tokenId)`: This function returns the address of the account that has transfer rights for the specified NFT (_tokenID).

`isApprovedForAll(address _owner, address _operator)`: This function checks whether one account (_operator) has transfer rights for all NFTs in another account (_owner).

`supportsInterface(bytes4 interfaceID)`: This function is included from the requisite ERC-165 interface for standard interface detection.

Now let's look at the events declared in the ERC-721 interface:

`Transfer(address indexed _from, address indexed _to, uint256 indexed _tokenId)`: This event must be emitted when NFTs are transferred from one account to another.

`Approval(address indexed _owner, address indexed _approved, uint256 indexed _tokenId)`: This event must be emitted each time an account approves an NFT transfer right to another account.

`ApprovalForAll(address indexed _owner, address indexed _operator, bool _approved)`: This event must be emitted whenever an account allows or disallows another account to access all of its NFTs.

In implementing the ERC-721 interface, some state variables must also be stored in the token contract. As before, the following state variables can be declared and defined however you see fit in your particular implementation of the interface.

owners[] stores the owner account address associated with each of the individual NFTs (this variable is an array).

balances[] stores the number of NFTs in each account (this variable is an array).

tokenApprovals[] stores the account address that is currently allowed transfer rights for each of the individual NFTs (this variable is an array).

operatorApprovals[][] tracks whether one account is currently allowed to transfer the NFTs from the other account (this variable is a matrix).

name (optional) stores the unifying group name for the NFTs (such as *CryptoKitties*).

symbol (optional) stores the symbol for the NFTs (such as CK in the case of CryptoKitties).

Again, different implementations may require additional functions or variables, which can be declared and defined as you see fit. To be ERC-721 compliant, however, all functions and events declared in the ERC-721 interface and ERC-165 interface must be named and implemented as specified by the interfaces.

Other token standards on Ethereum

With the proliferation of fungible and non-fungible tokens alike, varying implementations continue to provide added functionality and enhancements. Some of these features have been formalized as additional token standards, to provide either a new standard altogether (such as the multi-token standard) or a standard interface for improvements to the original fungible or non-fungible token interfaces.

Here are some examples of finalized standards:

>> **The ERC-777 Token Standard:** This standard introduced an interface for an ERC-20 backward-compatible fungible token with advanced features, some of which were popularized by the ERC-721 Non-Fungible Token Standard.

For instance, the ERC-777 interface specifies a function to grant an account the right to transfer tokens on behalf of another account.

>> **The ERC-1363 Payable Token Standard:** This standard introduced an interface for ERC-20 tokens to enable automatic code execution upon a successful call to the transfer, transferFrom, or approve functions.

>> **The ERC-2981 NFT Royalty Standard:** The ERC-2981 standard introduced an interface for ERC-721 and ERC-1155 non-fungible tokens to designate a royalty amount and recipient to be paid each time the NFT in question is sold.

>> **The ERC-1155 Multi-Token Standard:** This standard introduced a consolidated interface to manage fungible, non-fungible, and semi-fungible tokens (similar to limited-edition releases).

As adoption continues to spread and additional use cases materialize, you're sure to see more interesting and exciting token standards to come!

Chapter **11**

Building an ERC-721 Token

This chapter walks you through the steps in developing, compiling, and deploying your first non-fungible token contract.

To successfully follow the step-by-step guide in this chapter, you need to have completed some key steps in advance. We assume that you have faithfully followed the prerequisite hands-on instructional portions of Chapters 7, 8, and 9.

Writing and Compiling Your NFT

Because a token contract is a special type of smart contract, you begin your NFT journey with the steps for launching your first smart contract that we show you in Chapter 9. When in doubt, refer to that chapter for an illustrated guide on file creation and compilation.

The code

When building a token contract, always start by firing up the Remix environment — just follow these steps to get the ball rolling:

REMEMBER

1. **Go to** http://remix.ethereum.org.

   You must type http:// (without the *s*) and *not* https:// (with the *s*), or else Remix can't access MetaMask.

2. **Click the New File link under the File heading on the main page. (Alternatively, you can find the New File icon in the File Explorers pane, located on the left side of the page.)**

   A new file appears in the File Explorers pane, waiting for you to type a new name.

3. **Using the cursor, click into the blank text box, type NFTFD. sol, and then press Enter.**

   A new tab pops up, labeled with the name of the file.

REMEMBER

   The .sol extension is used to indicate a Solidity source file. For more on Solidity, see Chapter 9.

TIP

   At any time, click the Double Page icon, located on the toolbar running down the left side of the window, to return to the File Explorer browser pane.

4. **Type the following code into the newly created** NFTFD.sol **file:**

```solidity
pragma solidity ^0.8.0;

import "https://github.com/OpenZeppelin/
    openzeppelin-contracts/blob/master/
    contracts/token/ERC721/extensions/
    ERC721URIStorage.sol";

contract NFTFD is ERC721URIStorage {
    address public founder;

    constructor() ERC721("NFTs For Dummies",
    "NFTFD") {
        founder = msg.sender;
```

```
        for (uint tokenID=1; tokenID<=5;
tokenID++) {
            _mint(founder, tokenID);
            _setTokenURI(tokenID, "NFTFD
Limited Edition Initial Release");
        }
    }

    function mintNFT(
        address to,
        uint256 tokenID,
        string memory tokenURI
    )
        public
    {
        require(msg.sender == founder, "not
an authorized minter");
        _mint(to, tokenID);
        _setTokenURI(tokenID, tokenURI);
    }

}
```

WARNING

The `import "[...]/ERC721URIStorage.sol";` code line must be contained on a single line with no line breaks.

Avoid typos by directly copying and pasting this code from `www.seoyoungkim.com/nftfdcode.html`.

TIP

Solidity is case sensitive, so `ERC721URIStorage` and `erc721uristorage` aren't treated identically at compilation.

REMEMBER

5. **To compile the source code you just typed, click the Solidity-Compiler icon, located in the Navigation pane to the far left.**

You can find the Solidity Compiler icon just below the File Explorers Double Page icon.

6. **From the Solidity Compiler browser pane, click the Compile NFTFD.sol button.**

TIP

The compilation details for this contract appear underneath the Compile NFTFD.sol button. This time, when you click the Contract drop-down menu that appears (as shown in Figure 11-1), the following contract names appear in addition to NFTFD:

>> ERC721URIStorage

>> ERC721

>> IERC721

>> IERC721Receiver

>> IERC721Metadata

>> Address

>> Context

>> Strings

>> ERC165

>> IERC165

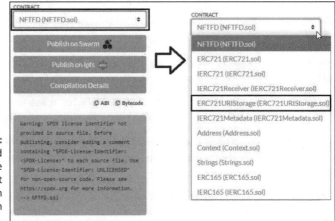

FIGURE 11-1:
NFTFD and base contract compilation details on Remix.

If you take a closer look at the source code we have you type in Step 4, you notice the line contract NFTFD is ERC721URI Storage {. It tells you that the NFTFD contract is directly *derived* from the prebuilt base contract — ERC721URIStorage (imported from https://github.com/OpenZeppelin/open zeppelin-contracts/blob/master/contracts/token/

ERC721/extensions/ERC721URIStorage.sol) — which is derived from the ERC721 base contract, which itself is derived from the other interfaces and contracts in the preceding list.

The play-by-play

The following is a chunk-by-chunk explanation of the NFTFD.sol code you use for your token contract. We also provide tips for whether you can easily customize elements of the code and not accidentally break something.

```
pragma solidity ^0.8.0;
```

I. This Solidity version pragma allows the source code to be compiled only under versions 0.8.x (including and following version 0.8.0 but strictly preceding version 0.9.0).

```
import "https://github.com/OpenZeppelin/
    openzeppelin-contracts/blob/master/contracts/
    token/ERC721/extensions/ERC721URIStorage.sol";
```

II. The next line of code directs the compiler to import the ERC721URIStorage contract from OpenZeppelin's smart-contract library. This contract serves as the base from which we derive our own token contract.

If you visit this particular URL to take a peek at the code in the ERC721URIStorage.sol file, you notice that ERC721URIStorage is itself derived from OpenZeppelin's ERC721 implementation, which is imported from https://github.com/OpenZeppelin/openzeppelin-contracts/blob/master/contracts/token/ERC721/ERC721.sol. The ERC721URIStorage contract provides enhanced functionality to ERC721 by adding a means to setting and storing additional token-specific information (*tokenURI*) for each token.

```
contract NFTFD is ERC721URIStorage {
```

III. Next, we define our contract, NFTFD. The code here, through the keyword is, specifies that our new contract is derived from a base contract, ERC721URIStorage, which is contained in the .sol file we imported in the prior line of code. This feature is known as *inheritance*. Solidity permits multiple inheritance. A contract can inherit numerous other contracts either indirectly or directly:

- » **Indirectly:** If our own NFTFD contract directly inherits from ERC721URIStorage, it also indirectly inherits from ERC721, a "parent" to ERC721URIStorage.

- » **Directly:** You can specify direct inheritance by providing a comma-separated list of all base contracts you want your contract to inherit from.

TIP

You can type a name for your token contract that's different from NFTFD, which we've chosen, without having to alter other elements of the instructions or code to conform to your chosen contract name.

```
address public founder;
```

IV. This line declares a public state variable, founder, of type address. In the code the follows, this variable is assigned the account address of the token's founder, and is used to ensure that only the founder's account has the ability to mint new tokens.

```
constructor() ERC721("NFTs For Dummies", "NFTFD")
    {
```

V. This block of code declares the special constructor() function, which is executed just once at contract initiation. Notice the additional statement in the declaration: ERC721("NFTs For Dummies", "NFTFD"). This portion specifies the name and ticker, respectively, to be used in the ERC721's constructor function.

TIP

You can customize the name of, and ticker for, your token to whatever you want without having to worry about remaining compatible with other parts of the code. Simply type a name and ticker to replace the strings "NFTs For Dummies" and "NFTFD" in the preceding constructor() declaration.

```
founder = msg.sender;
```

VI. Turning to the contents of the `constructor()` function, the first line of code (within the function's defining curly brackets) initializes the address being stored in the `founder` state variable as `msg.sender`, which contains the address of the account that has initiated the transaction. Specifically, `msg` is a global variable that contains information about the current transaction, and `sender` is a member of this object (known as a *struct* in Solidity). Because this code is part of the `constructor()` function, this line of code essentially stores the address of the account from which the token contract is deployed in the `founder` state variable.

```
for (uint tokenID=1; tokenID<=5; tokenID++) {
    _mint(founder, tokenID);
    _setTokenURI(tokenID, "NFTFD Limited
Edition Initial Release");
  }
```

VII. The next block of code implements a `for` loop that iteratively creates new tokens, numbered: 1, 2, 3, 4, and 5.

You can customize how many tokens to create by simply changing the number "5" in the `tokenID<=5` portion of the code defining the `for` loop. *Be careful!* Selecting a large number dramatically increases the time and gas required to deploy your token contract.

Within this `for` loop, the `_mint(founder, tokenID)` function call creates a new token, with numeric identifier `tokenID`, and designates the `founder` address as the account owning this new token. The `_setTokenURI(tokenID, "NFTFD Limited Edition Initial Release")` function call stores the string "NFTFD Limited Edition Initial Release" as part of the token-specific information that can later be accessed for the token with numeric identifier `tokenID`. The `_mint` and `_setTokenURI` functions are originally defined in base contracts `ERC721` and `ERC721URIStorage`, respectively.

You can customize the string you want to store in place of "NFTFD Limited Edition Initial Release" by typing your own string in its place.

```
}
```

VIII. Next, you complete the constructor() function with a closing curly bracket before moving on to define the next function.

```
function mintNFT(
    address to,
    uint256 tokenID,
    string memory tokenURI
)
    public
```

IX. This block of code declares a public function, mintNFT(), that accepts three arguments: to, tokenID, and tokenURI, whose respective types are address, uint256, and string.

```
{
    require(msg.sender == founder, "not an
authorized minter");
    _mint(to, tokenID);
    _setTokenURI(tokenID, tokenURI);
}
```

X. This block of code implements the mintNFT() function.

The first line specifies a requirement that must be fulfilled for the remaining code to be executed. Here, this built-in Solidity function, require, determines whether the account issuing the mintNFT(to, tokenID, tokenURI) function call is the authorized founder. If this condition isn't satisfied, the unauthorized function caller receives the message "not an authorized minter" and the function call terminates without further execution.

Assuming that this condition is satisfied, the _mint(to, tokenID) function call creates a new token, with numeric identifier tokenID, and designates the to address as the account owning this new token. Then the _setTokenURI(tokenID, tokenURI) function call stores the string in tokenURI as part of the token-specific information that can later be accessed for the token with numeric identifier tokenID.

```
}
```

XI. And, of course, you complete the block of contract code with a closing curly bracket.

Deploying Your NFT

After you've entered and compiled your source code, you can put the bytecode into action!

TIP

Before proceeding, it may be helpful for you to refer to Chapters 7 and 8 for an illustrated refresher on switching networks and switching accounts on MetaMask. You may also want to refer to Chapter 9 for an illustrated refresher on deploying your smart contract.

Deploying on Ganache

We start by deploying our token contract on our local Ganache environment.

REMEMBER

Have the Ganache desktop application open and running the appropriate workspace — in our case, the Handsomely-Vessel workspace (see Chapter 8), which we've been using throughout our step-by-step guide:

1. **Sign in to your MetaMask browser extension.**

2. **Connect to the Handsomely-Vessel custom network and select one of your imported local Ganache accounts by clicking the colorful circle in the upper-right corner of the MetaMask interface.**

   In our case, we continue to use Ganache HV1, beginning with account address 0x655E [. . .], as shown in Figure 11-2.

3. **From the Remix browser page, click the Ethereum icon on the navigation pane on the far left to navigate to the Deploy & Run Transactions browser pane.**

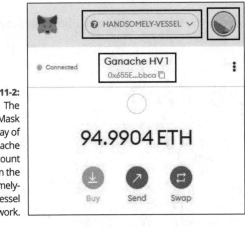

FIGURE 11-2:
The MetaMask display of the Ganache HV1 account on the Handsomely-Vessel network.

4. **Select the Injected Web3 option from the Environment drop-down menu.**

   Your selected account appears on the Account drop-down menu (in our case, beginning with account address "0x655E[. . .]"), as shown in Figure 11-3.

5. **Select the compiled** NFTFD **contract from the Contract drop-down menu and then click the Deploy button.**

6. **Click the Confirm button on the MetaMask pop-up notification to proceed.**

FIGURE 11-3:
Selected Ganache Environment and Account on Remix.

Great! You have now successfully deployed NFTFD to your local Handsomely-Vessel blockchain. Of course, this occurred rather quickly, given that Ganache automatically mines blocks to allow for swift testing and exploration.

Below the Deploy button on the Deploy & Run Transactions browser pane is your deployed contract NFTFD along with its public functions and data, as shown in Figure 11-4.

Public functions and data of the NFTFD contract.

TECHNICAL STUFF

Aside from the mintNFT function and founder state variable (which we describe in the section "The play-by-play" earlier in this chapter), the remaining contract features are part of the standard ERC-721 interface. (See Chapter 10.)

This menu allows you to interact with your newly deployed token contract. Some interactions are free, and others require gas. Play around and see what you discover. We go into greater detail — and provide more illustrations — as you graduate to the Ropsten Testnet!

Deploying on Ropsten

You now need to switch gears in order to make your way to the Ropsten Test Network.

First connect to the Ropsten Test Network from your MetaMask wallet and then select an account that has Ropsten test ETH (which we show you how to create and fund in Chapter 7). In our case, we continue to use our Testnet account, with account address 0x43371B75585785D62e3a50533aa15ee8D350273F, as shown in Figure 11-5.

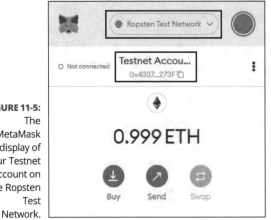

FIGURE 11-5: The MetaMask display of our Testnet account on the Ropsten Test Network.

Toggling back to the Deploy & Run Transactions pane on the Remix browser page, execute the following steps:

1. Select the Injected Web3 option from the Environment drop-down menu.

The account you've selected on MetaMask appears on the Account drop-down menu (in our case, 0x43371B75585785 D62e3a50533aa15ee8D350273F), as shown in Figure 11-6.

2. Select the compiled NFTFD contract from the Contract drop-down menu, and then click the Deploy button.

3. Click the Confirm button on the MetaMask pop-up notification to proceed, as shown in Figure 11-7.

FIGURE 11-6:
The selected
Ropsten
environ-
ment and
account on
Remix.

FIGURE 11-7:
Confirming
contract
deployment
on the
Ropsten
Test
Network.

Excellent! Once your transaction is executed on Ropsten, another contract appears under the Deployed Contracts list on the Deploy & Run Transactions page. Click the Double Page icon to the right of your contract's name, as shown in Figure 11-8, to save the contract address.

Our contract's address is 0xd4139A846b5561c31df03FbbCE358 3f1A7d8A814. Later, we discuss how to use this address to continue to track and interact with your contract.

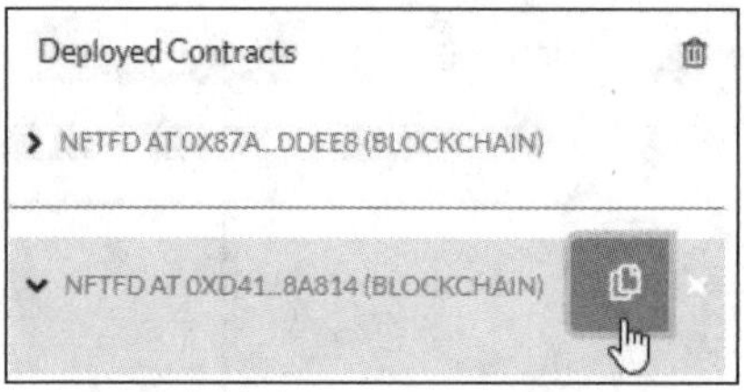

FIGURE 11-8: Copying your newly deployed contract's address.

WARNING

The wait time to execution is typically less than one minute, but there can be quite a lot of variation in execution times. Be patient! If the network remains unresponsive for more than ten minutes, take a short break and try again.

As before, when you deployed your `NFTFD` contract on your local Ganache blockchain earlier in this chapter, notice the same list of public functions and data under the `NFTFD` contract you just deployed on Ropsten.

For instance, if you click the Founder button, you see the address of the account from which the token contract was deployed. You can also paste this address into the balanceOf input box, which shows five tokens in this account, as shown in Figure 11-9. (Recall that our code generated five tokens at initiation.) These data calls don't require gas.

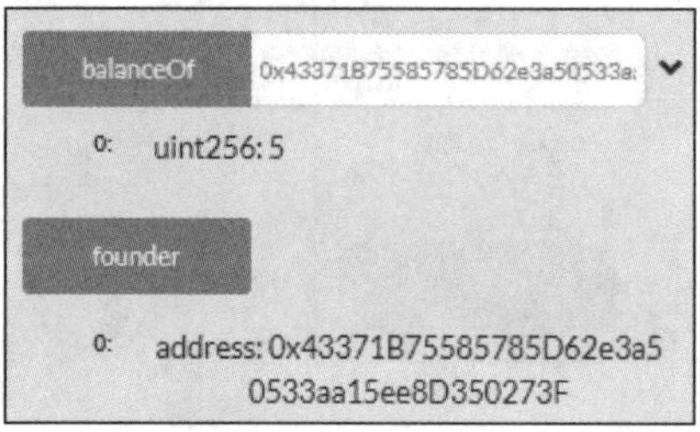

FIGURE 11-9: Interacting with `NFTFD` deployed on Ropsten.

If you continue to interact with this contract from the founder account, you can use the mintNFT button to create a new NFTFD token. (Note that creating a new token does require gas.) Here's how that's done:

1. **Click the downward arrow to the right of the mintNFT button, as shown in Figure 11-10.**

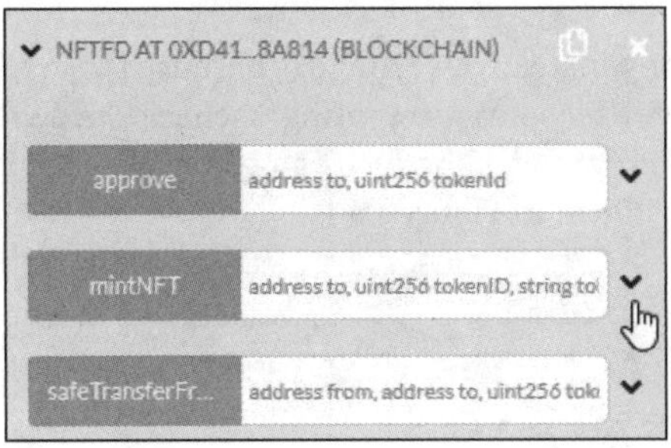

FIGURE 11-10:
Expanding
function
parameters
housed in
our NFTFD
contract.

2. **Fill in the function parameters as follows, as shown in Figure 11-11:**

   a. `to: 0x885b0F6065B2cD6655eDcc2F7A12062b1ca79d97`

      This address links to another test account we created via MetaMask. You can use whatever account address you want here. To prevent confusion, however, we strongly recommend that you avoid co-mingling digital assets across different networks within the same account (as we discuss in Chapter 7).

   b. `tokenID: 17760704`

   c. `tokenURI: https://en.wikipedia.org/wiki/Independence_Day_(United_States)`

3. **Click the Transact button, and then click the Confirm button on the MetaMask pop-up notification.**

FIGURE 11-11:
Your
`mintNFT`
function
parameters.

Excellent! You've now created and gifted a new NFTFD token.

You can verify the owner and URI of this token by typing **17760704** (the `tokenID` inputted in Step 2 of the preceding example) in the input boxes next to the ownerOf and tokenURI buttons, as shown in Figure 11-12. This information changes if you type **1** or **5** instead of **17760704**, because those tokens belong to the founder account. Attempting to check the owner of a non-existent token number produces an error message in the Remix console, as shown in Figure 11-13.

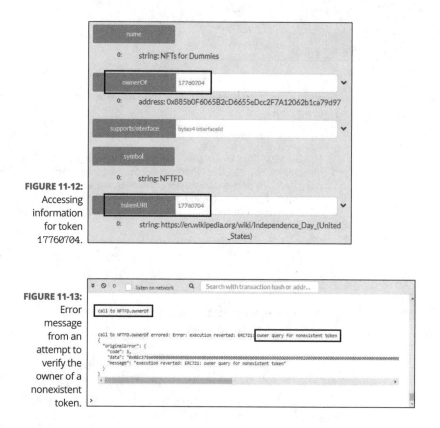

FIGURE 11-12:
Accessing
information
for token
17760704.

FIGURE 11-13:
Error
message
from an
attempt to
verify the
owner of a
nonexistent
token.

You can also track your new NFTFD token holdings via your MetaMask wallet. Make sure you're on the right account and Ropsten Test Network within your MetaMask wallet. We start with the Testnet account (0x43371B75585785D62e3a50533aa15e e8D350273F) that we use to deploy the NFTFD contract, and proceed on MetaMask as follows:

1. Click the **Assets tab** (toward the bottom of the account screen) and then click the **Add Token** button, as shown in Figure 11-14.

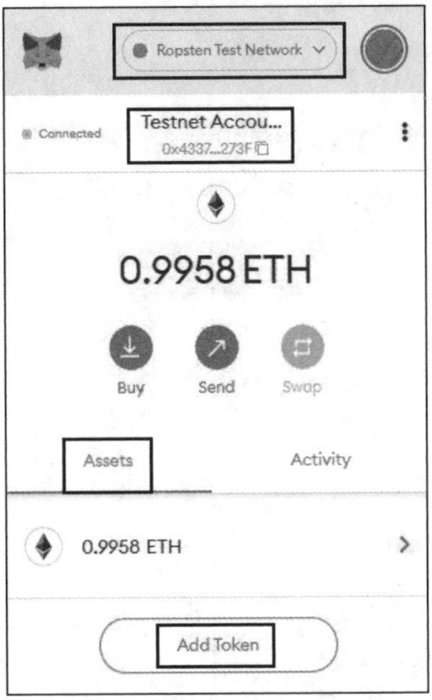

FIGURE 11-14: Adding a new token type on your MetaMask wallet.

2. On the Add Tokens page that appears (see Figure 11-15), type the appropriate Token contract address.

In our case, it's 0xd4139A846b5561c31df03FbbCE–3583f1A7d8A814.

The Token Symbol field automatically displays NFTFD after the contract address has been entered.

3. Enter 0 for Token Decimal and then click the Next button.

The next page shows the token being added (NFTFD) and the token balance for this particular account.

Unlike fungible tokens, each NFT is unique and cannot be further divided (see Chapter 1). Thus, the "Token Decimal" field is set to "0" for NFTs.

REMEMBER

4. Click the Add Tokens button, as shown in Figure 11-16.

Now whenever you toggle to see the assets in your account, you see the five NFTFD in addition to the test ETH, as shown in Figure 11-17.

FIGURE 11-15: Specifying the custom details for a new token type on your MetaMask wallet.

FIGURE 11-16: Finalizing a new token type and its account balance on your MetaMask wallet.

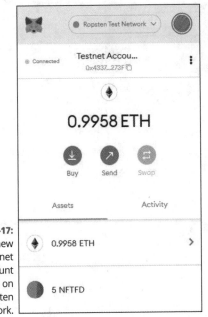

FIGURE 11-17:
Our new
Testnet
account
balance on
the Ropsten
Test Network.

REMEMBER

In line with our discussion on "disappearing" balances in Chapter 7, the NFTFD balance in our Testnet Account appears only when we're connected to the Ropsten Test Network, because this NFTFD token contract (0xd4139A846b5561c31df03FbbC E3583f1A7d8A814) was deployed on Ropsten and doesn't exist on other networks.

For instance, both the test ETH balance and the NFTFD balance entirely disappear when you view our Testnet account while connected to the Ethereum Mainnet, as shown in Figure 11-18.

For the sake of completeness, we reexecute the previous steps to add the NFTFD token balance to our second test account, 0x885b0F6065B2cD6655eDcc2F7A12062b1ca79d97, which was given the special 17760704 token that we minted after contract initiation. As expected, MetaMask displays an NFTFD balance of 1 on this account, as shown in Figure 11-19.

FIGURE 11-18:
Our Testnet account balance on the Ethereum Mainnet.

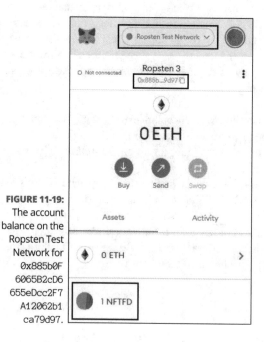

FIGURE 11-19:
The account balance on the Ropsten Test Network for 0x885b0F 6065B2cD6 655eDcc2F7 A12062b1 ca79d97.

To keep things straight, here's a summary of the various addresses referenced and the tokens created:

>> **The account from which we deployed the NFTFD contract on Ropsten:** 0x43371B75585785D62e3a50533aa 15ee8D350273F

>> **A second account:** 0x885b0F6065B2cD6655e Dcc2F7A12062b1ca79d97, which was gifted the specially minted token with tokenID 17760704

>> **The NFTFD contract account on Ropsten:** 0xd4139A846b5561c31df03FbbCE3583f1A7d8A814

>> **A total of six NFTFDs:** 1, 2, 3, 4, 5, and 17760704

Of these, tokens 1, 2, 3, 4, and 5 were created at contract initiation, with URI NFTFD Limited Edition Initial Release, and held by the founder: 0x43371B75585785D62e3a50533 aa15ee8D350273F

The sixth token, 17760704, was minted by the founder account after contract initiation and held by another account: 0x885b0F6065B2cD6655eDcc2F7A12062 b1ca79d97

The most important information to note is the contract account address, which you need if you want to later track or continue to interact with this contract from time to time.

Deploying on Mainnet

If you have the ETH to burn, you can also deploy your token contract on the Ethereum Mainnet.

The steps to deploy on Mainnet are nearly identical to the steps we covered previously to deploy on Ropsten. The main difference is that you need to be connected to the Ethereum Mainnet with an account funded with some actual ETH.

In addition, when you attempt to deploy your contract on Mainnet, Remix presents a pop-up warning, as shown in Figure 11-20, to ensure that you're aware you're creating a transaction on Mainnet.

Confirm transaction ✕

You are about to create a transaction on Main Network. Confirm the details to send the info to your provider.
The provider for many users is MetaMask. The provider will ask you to sign the transaction before it is sent to Main Network.

From: 0xde992fee80edccdf3875aba569b0f1ac87daab34
To: (Contract Creation)
Data: 0x6080604052348015620000115760008000fd5b50604051806...
Amount: 0 Ether

Gas estimation: 3078892
Gas limit: 3078892
Max Priority fee: [0] Gwei
Max fee (Not less than base fee 65.554680462 Gwei): [65.554680] Gwei
Max transaction fee: 0.201835781237008104 Ether

☐ Do not show this warning again.

[Confirm] [Cancel]

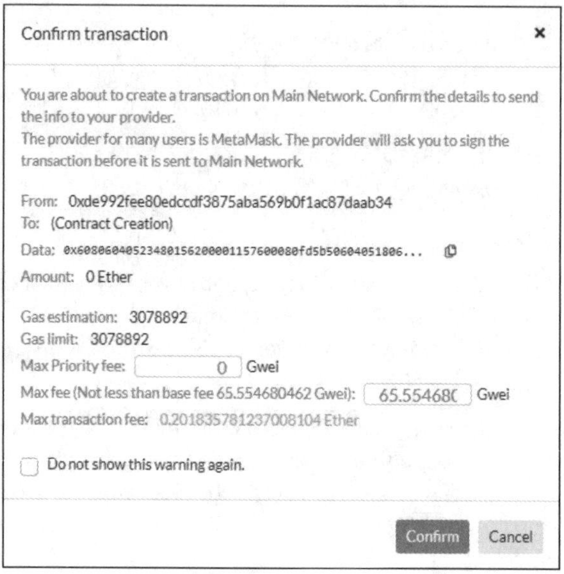

FIGURE 11-20: Warning on Remix when attempting to create a transaction on Mainnet.

If you click the Confirm button, a MetaMask notification appears, outlining the estimated gas fees for contract deployment, as shown in Figure 11-21. This notification is similar to the one provided for contract deployment on Ropsten (refer to Figure 11-7), except that MetaMask now also provides the estimated USD equivalent of the ETH being spent. Here, the suggested gas fee to deploy our NFTFD contract on Mainnet is 0.202058 ETH ($642.44 USD). (Alas, we do not have sufficient funds to deploy to Mainnet.)

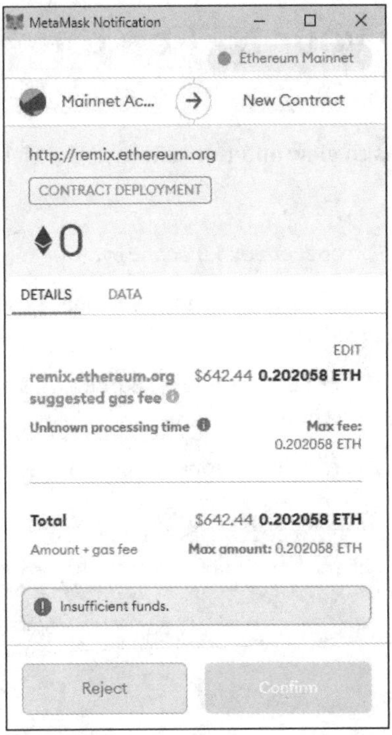

FIGURE 11-21: Estimated gas fee and USD equivalent to deploy our NFTFD contract on Mainnet.

Nurturing Your NFT

Once you've deployed your first NFT, you can continue to track and interact with this contract going forward.

For simplicity's sake, we outline our steps to track the NFTFD contract we deployed on the Ropsten Test Network (with the contract address 0xd4139A846b5561c31df03FbbCE3583f1A7d 8A814).

REMEMBER

The steps to tracking and interacting with a contract deployed on Mainnet are nearly identical, and we note these differences as we walk you through the steps in the following section.

Following your NFT on the blockchain

Follow these steps to view all information and activity related to your NFT:

1. **Go to** `https://ropsten.etherscan.io`.

   Note: To view a contract deployed on Mainnet, go to `https://etherscan.io`.

2. **Paste the contract address in the search bar, shown in Figure 11-22, and then press Enter.**

   Alternatively, you can simply append your contract address to `https://ropsten.etherscan.io/address`. In our case, we get this: `https://ropsten.etherscan.io/address/0xd4139A846b5561c31df03FbbCE3583f1A7d8A814`.

FIGURE 11-22:
Finding your
contract on
Ropsten.

   A page appears, showing information regarding the contract creator, the transactions associated with this contract, and the contract events that have been logged.

3. **Click the link in the Token Tracker field under the More Info box, located in the upper-right corner, as shown in Figure 11-23.**

   Alternatively, you can simply append your contract address to `https://ropsten.etherscan.io/token`. In our case, we get `https://ropsten.etherscan.io/token/0xd4139A846b5561c31df03FbbCE3583f1A7d8A814`.

   A page appears, showing information regarding token transfers and holdings.

FIGURE 11-23:
A basic
contract
profile
provided by
Etherscan.

For instance, you can see a total of six transactions on the
Transfers information tab, as shown in Figure 11-24. Here,
notice tokens 1, 2, 3, 4, and 5, which were assigned to the
founder account (0x43371B75585785D62e3a50533aa15ee
8D350273F), and the subsequently minted token 17760704,
which was assigned to a separate account
(0x885b0F6065B2cD6655eDcc2F7A12062b1ca79d97).

Under the Holders tab, as shown in Figure 11-25, you can
see all token holders in this particular token economy, along
with their respective token balances.

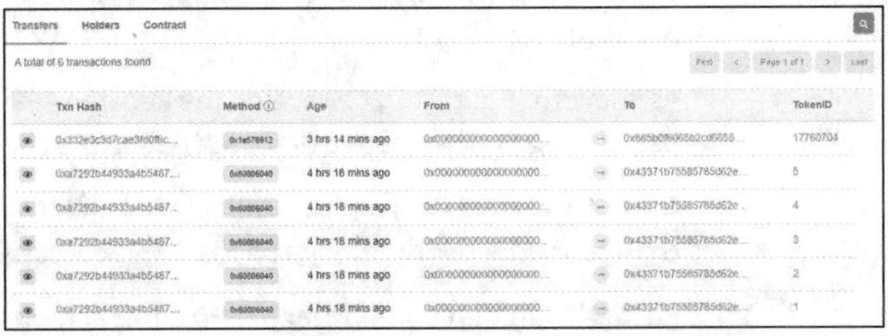

FIGURE 11-24:
NFTFD token-
transfer
information
provided by
Etherscan.

That means you can track all transactions and changes as your
token economy grows!

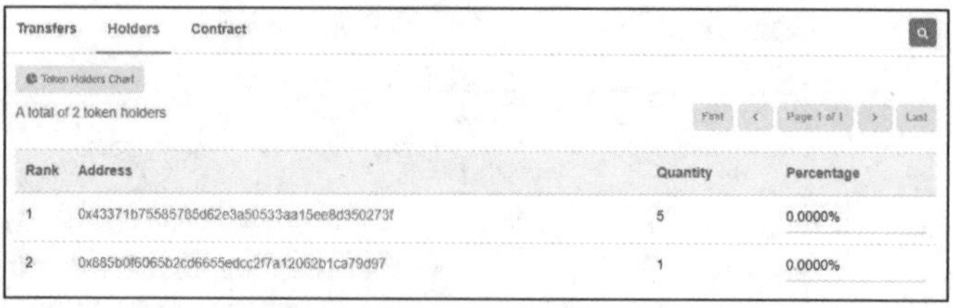
Transfers
Holders
Contract
Token Holders Chart
A total of 2 token holders
First
Page 1 of 1
Last
Rank
Address
Quantity
Percentage
1
0x43371b75585785d62e3a50533aa15ee8d350273f
5
0.0000%
2
0x885b0f6065b2cd6655edcc2f7a12062b1ca79d97
1
0.0000%

FIGURE 11-25: NFTFD token-holder information provided by Etherscan.

Interacting with your NFT

If you want to interact with your NFT again later (perhaps to mint additional tokens), you need to recompile your contract code and return to the Deploy & Run Transactions page on Remix:

1. **Log in to your MetaMask wallet, with the appropriate account and network.**
2. **Go to** `http://remix.ethereum.org`**.**
3. **Double-click the** `NFTFD.sol` **file to open the contract code created earlier and compile the source code from the "Solidity Compiler" pane.**
4. **Click the Ethereum icon located on the navigation pane to the far left to access the Deploy & Run Transactions page.**
5. **Select Injected Web3 to change your environment, and ensure you're connected to the appropriate network and account.**

   As shown in Figure 11-26, we're on the Ropsten Test Network because that's where we've deployed our `NFTFD` contract.

   Note: To interact with a contract deployed on Mainnet, change your network settings on MetaMask accordingly.
6. **Rather than deploy another** `NFTFD` **contract, paste in your contract's address at the At Address prompt, located toward the bottom of the Deploy & Run Transactions page, also shown in Figure 11-26, and press Enter.**

   In our case, we proceed to look up our contract: `0xd4139A846b5561c31df03FbbCE3583f1A7d8A814`

   This contract appears in the list of deployed contracts, as shown in Figure 11-27.

Ta-da! You can now proceed to mint additional tokens, transfer existing tokens, or simply access basic data stored in the `NFTFD` contract.

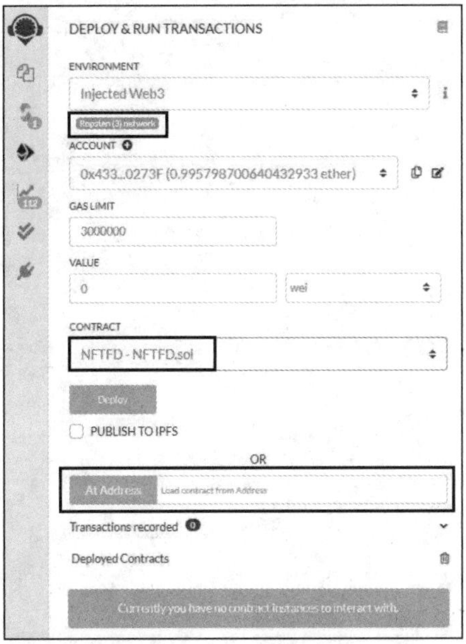

FIGURE 11-26:
Locating the
previously
deployed
NFTFD
contract.

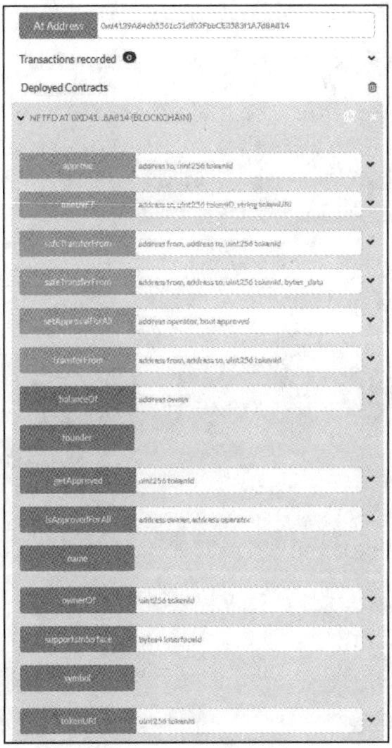

FIGURE 11-27:
Interacting
with NFTFD
(again).

The Part of Tens

4

IN THIS PART . . .

Discover the ten fastest-growing NFT platforms.

Explore the ten most expensive NFTs of all time.

Chapter **12**

Ten Marketplaces for Your NFTs

NFTs have taken the world by storm, and the NFT space is evolving *quickly*. This chapter uncovers the top ten most exciting platforms to create and collect NFTs. You can evaluate the features and drawbacks of each platform described here so that you can become better prepared to create, trade, and collect NFTs.

The NFT is a huge economic invention — it allows creatives anywhere in the world to create and share their creations while still collecting payment for their hard work. This economic opportunity took off in part because of the economic conditions that COVID created in 2020, but now that artist and collector have been empowered with this new technology, it's unlikely to fade out.

The OpenSea Marketplace

The OpenSea marketplace (https://opensea.io) is the first and largest peer-to-peer platform for cryptocollectibles. Active since 2018, it's one of the world's most popular NFT markets. (Peer-to-peer platforms are controlled by the contributors to the ecosystem, much like a co-op.)

OpenSea has many tools that allow

>> Consumers to trade their assets freely

>> Creators to launch new digital works

>> Developers to build rich, integrated marketplaces for their digital assets

The platform is user-friendly — all you have to do to add your own NFT to the mix is specify a few categories and upload your artwork. The ownership of the token is assigned after creation, enabling you to immediately sell or transfer on this marketplace. OpenSea is compatible with open blockchain standards, which means you can create your work on another platform and then list it on OpenSea. You can do all this without paying listing fees or enduring an exhaustive listing process — though OpenSea does make money when you sell.

How much money? Well, whenever someone buys an NFT on OpenSea, the company gets a cut of 2.5 percent of the NFT's sale price. The original creator of the NFT can also choose to take a fee on subsequent sales of their artwork. In effect, they can create a royalty stream for themselves.

The downside of OpenSea is that it doesn't allow purchases by credit card or PayPal. You need to own crypto already, or purchase some, to be able to use the marketplace.

The upside is that OpenSea has a referral affiliate program: If you refer a friend to OpenSea who makes a purchase, you can earn between 40 percent and 100 percent of the fee that OpenSea receives for that sale.

The Axie Infinity Marketplace

The Axie Infinity marketplace (`https://axieinfinity.com`) supports the Axie Infinity online video game, developed by Vietnamese studio Sky Mavis. This marketplace sells characters and items only from the Axie Infinity ecosystem, but it's still one of the most popular NFT marketplaces in the world.

In Axie Infinity, which was inspired by Pokémon, you earn tokens via gameplay and contributions to the ecosystem. It has two cryptocurrencies: Axie Infinity Shards (AXS) and Small Love Potion (SLP). The game currencies are used to battle, collect, raise, and build a land-based kingdom for your Axie pets in gameplay.

The critical difference between Axie Infinity and a traditional game is that it has player-centric economics. The system rewards players for their contributions to the ecosystem. (If you're a fan of the novel *Ready Player One*, you know what we're talking about.) This new gaming model, called *Play-to-Earn*, has been hypothesized as a viable economic system in a post-scarcity world. Axie has attracted thousands of players from developing countries who are looking for new income streams during the COVID pandemic.

When you trade on the Axie Infinity marketplace, the seller pays a 4.25 percent fee. The Sky Mavis team has used these fees to fund further development. However, the marketplace fees will go to a community treasury that rewards AXS token holders via *staking* — taking your tokens and locking them in a smart contract that then pays you a dividend in the same cryptocurrency. It works similar to a CD or savings account.

Like OpenSea, the Axie Infinity Marketplace doesn't support PayPal or credit card payments. You can use your MetaMask wallet (see Chapter 2) for smaller transactions or exchanges like Coinbase (`www.coinbase.com`) for larger transactions. Large and small transaction will mean different things to different people. It has to do with your desire for convenience versus security. When I refer to a small transaction, it would be equivalent to what I would be willing have in cash on me at any time. Large transaction are rare and its ok if I need to go through a few more security hurtles in order to protect my funds.

The CryptoPunks Marketplace

Launched in June 2017, *CryptoPunks* (www.larvalabs.com/cryptopunks) is one of the earliest non-fungible token marketplaces. Developed by Larva Labs (based in New York City), *CryptoPunks* was built on the Ethereum blockchain network and features 10,000 unique 24-x-24 pixel art images — reminiscent of early video game art — which are generated algorithmically. Every piece has its own profile page stating its attributes and ownership status.

In the beginning, *CryptoPunks* could be claimable by anyone with an Ethereum wallet. However, now they're sold for millions of dollars. For example, "CryptoPunk #7523" sold for $11,754,000 as part of Sotheby's online auction "Natively Digital: A Curated NFT Sale."

The images of the *CryptoPunks* are too big to store economically on Ethereum. The image that the NFT represents is hashed. It's the hash that's written to the blockchain.

REMEMBER

A cryptographic hash function (introduced in Chapter 6) is an algorithm that uses an arbitrary amount of data — a *CryptoPunks* picture, for example — to create a small, fixed-size, unique string of characters. Data scientists have used hashes for years to manage large amounts of digital information, like the 10,000 unique *CryptoPunks*.

TECHNICAL STUFF

You can verify your *CryptoPunks* by checking the Ethereum smart contract and calculating an SHA-256 hash on the *s* image and comparing it to the hash stored in the contract.

You can get your own *CryptoPunks* by following these steps:

1. **If you haven't done so already, download and install MetaMask, a plugin for the Chrome browser.**

   For more on MetaMask, see Chapter 2.

2. **Buy some Ether or transfer some from another account.**

3. **Point your Chrome browser to** www.larvalabs.com/cryptopunks/forsale.

4. **Log in with your MetaMask plugin.**

After recognizing your wallet, the Larva Labs website adds buttons to the interface that allow you to bid on, buy, and sell *CryptoPunks* directly from your browser.

The NBA Top Shot Marketplace

In 2019, the NBA partnered with Dapperlabs, the creators of *CryptoKitties*, to create the Top Shot marketplace (https://nbatopshot.com). The subsequent licensing agreement with the NBA and its players' union has been wildly popular and produced hundreds of millions in sales in just the first year.

REMEMBER

A significant characteristic of the digital era is that information can be endlessly replicated and shared. Scarcity has been difficult to regulate on the Internet. Pirated information is easily accessible and free. The revolution of blockchain technology was its ability to create digital scarcity and authenticity at a negligible cost. Now industries like sports memorabilia can reinvent themselves in a digital world.

Replicating the media file an NFT represents is possible, but it's difficult to change the ownership record of the NFT — as long as adequate security has been used, to be clear. This is because the item has been secured within the blockchain's distributed network. Investors are buying up sports NFTs because they believe this new type of sports memorabilia will continue to have collectors — acting in ways much like old school basketball, baseball, and football cards.

Top Shot offers four tiers of collectibles that allow you to purchase common editions (1 in 10,000) all the way up to an ultimate edition (1 of 1). Top Shot charges a 5.00 percent fee, which is split between Dapper and the NBA at purchase. Buying NFTs on NBA Top Shot is straightforward and easy because the marketplace allows purchases by credit card as well as cryptocurrency, and it has a user-friendly website.

The Rarible Marketplace

Rarible (`https://rarible.com`) launched in 2020 and quickly rose in popularity to become one of the largest NFT marketplaces, raking in some $150 million in sales in 18 months. Every type of NFT you can imagine is available for purchase because Rarible allows anyone to buy and auction off digital art. Rarible also has a governance token that enables users to make and vote on proposals around the platform's features and fees. (For more on governance tokens, see Chapter 4.)

The self-listing process has created a lot of diversity in the supply of NFTs, which can be a bit overwhelming when you're just starting. As a content creator on Rarible, you can decide to sell your NFTs in one of two ways: the Buy Now option or the auction.

As a buyer, you can sort and filter the NFTs using a wide assortment of categories, ensuring that you find a niche you love. At Rarible, you pay 2.50 percent to the marketplace as a commission, but no listing fees are involved for artists or investors. The original creator of the NFT can also choose to take additional fees on the future sale of their creations. Rarible doesn't work with credit cards or PayPal. If you want to purchase items, you have to use the MetaMask wallet we show you how to install in Chapter 2 or transfer crypto from another wallet.

REMEMBER

As on most crypto websites, you can engage with the website by way of an Ethereum wallet plugin on your web browser. As of this writing, MetaMask (a Chrome browser plugin) provides you with the best user experience. After you have access to your Ethereum wallet, connect it to Rarible and then follow these steps to fill out your profile:

1. **Navigate to** `https://rarible.com/`.

2. **Click the Sign In button.**

3. **In the new page that appears, click the Sign In with MetaMask button.**

4. **Click the My Profile button in the pull-down menu.**

5. **Click the Edit Profile button.**

6. **Add a profile picture and a cover image.**

7. **Enter your account information.**

8. **(Optional) Link your social media accounts to share your collection.**

9. **(Optional) Set a custom URL.**

After all that, you're able to create new NFTs or start collecting ones you love.

SuperRare Marketplace

At the SuperRare marketplace (`https://superrare.com/market`), you can collect and trade single-edition digital artworks that have been secured on the Ethereum blockchain with an ER721 token. This marketplace features beautiful and often head-scratching collections. Active since 2018, the US-based SuperRare uses the Ethereum Network, and its NFTs are the common ERC-721 token type.

SuperRare is more selective about who's allowed to sell NFTs on its platform, positioning itself as the Christie's auction house of the NFT world. Each NFT backs an official piece of digital art created by an artist from its network. You need cryptocurrency to buy items on SuperRare, and all transactions are made using Ether, Ethereum's native token. (`Coinbase.com` is an easy place to buy ether using a bank account.)

Here's a breakdown of how transactions work on SuperRare:

>> **All purchases:** The buyer pays a 3 percent transaction fee.

>> **Primary sales:** The buyer pays a 15 percent commission; secondary sales carry a 10 percent royalty.

>> **Beta Launch Artwork:** NFTs with a token ID lower than 4,000 are from the beta launch and have a different locked-in fee rate. These early works have no transaction fee or commission on primary sales, and a 3% commission on secondary sales.

SuperRare sees secondary fees as the best way to support artists and one of the artist community's best innovations.

The Alcor NFT Marketplace

Alcor (https://greymass.com/en) is much more than just another NFT marketplace. Launched in 2020, its decentralized exchanges (DEX) act as peer-to-peer (P2P) marketplaces connecting NFT buyers and sellers. Decentralized platforms are *noncustodial*, which means users remain in control of their private keys — better for power users and maybe a bit harder to manage as a beginner. Regardless, Alcor's flexible platform allows *self-listing*, or letting artists list themselves for free, and they can sell their artwork directly. Alcor also offers zero-fee NFT trading.

TECHNICAL STUFF

Alcor has been one fast-growing DEX on the Internet. Unlike most NFT marketplaces, Alcor was built on EOSIO blockchain and has integrations with BOS, EOS, Proton, TELOS, and WAX blockchains. You can do a ton of things using Alcor that extend way beyond NFT creation and listing. For example, you can also create:

>> **Liquidity pools for tokens:** This is where tokens are locked in smart contracts that provide liquidity in decentralized exchanges.

>> **Limit/market trading for cryptocurrencies:** This is a trading strategy to help with market volatility.

>> **Tokens:** These can be used to issue equity or represent other types of assets.

>> **Market pairs:** This is a market neutral trading strategy that allows you to profit from virtually any market condition.

TIP

Alcor doesn't allow withdrawals or deposits with a credit card or PayPal, and MetaMask doesn't work on the Alcor website. To use Alcor, you need an Anchor wallet (https://greymass.com/en/anchor/download), available in both mobile and desktop versions that enable you to log in, sign documents, and execute distributed smart contracts.

If you go with the Anchor wallet for your phone, it stores your private keys with military-grade encryption using the secure enclave tied to the biometric information on your smartphone.

An *enclave* is an area isolated from the main processor to provide an extra layer of security. It is designed to keep sensitive user data secure.

The Binance NFT Marketplace

The Chinese cryptocurrency exchange Binance (`www.binance.com`) created an NFT exchange in 2021, launching with artwork by the legendary artists Andy Warhol and Salvador Dali. Binance lists all types of NFTs, including sports and e-sports items, collectibles, entertainment items, and digital art. The marketplace operates on the Binance Smart Chain using BEP-721 tokens, a token standard for Binance. The Binance NFT marketplace also supports NFTs on the Ethereum network.

NFTs created on either Binance Smart Chain or Ethereum are subject to blockchain network fees. In addition to these fees, NFTs made on Binance's NFT marketplace are subject to a 1 percent listing fee paid in Binance Coin (BNB). As an artist, you can choose from an auction or fixed-price format, and you can take payment in one of several different cryptocurrencies. Artists receive a 1 percent royalty payment for any subsequent trading of their NFT on the platform. If you transfer in an NFT you own, you can also receive a 1 percent royalty when it's sold. Currently, there is not a universally recognized token standard that guarantees royalties outside of the platform they have been issued on. However, this is likely to change in the near future.

Making an NFT on Binance is straightforward. After you enter the basic details about your NFT and the type and length of the sale, the Binance team reviews your submission before listing it.

The Binance NFT marketplace is connected to its exchange, making it a little easier to get your hands on NFTs. You can deposit money into your exchange account with a wire transfer or debit card and then use those funds to buy NFTs.

Never leave large sums of money on an exchange — they're vulnerable to attack.

The Foundation NFT Marketplace

The Foundation NFT marketplace (https://foundation.app) is building a new creative economy for artists, creators, and collectors. As with other NFT marketplaces, creatives who make use of the Foundation platform are compensated for their work and build stronger connections with their supporters. The Foundation launched in 2021 and had hundreds of millions in sales within months.

To start collecting NFTs, go to Foundation's home page, click Connect Wallet, and then choose MetaMask from the menu that appears. After linking MetaMask, you can log on to the marketplace area of the Foundation website.

NFTs on the Foundation marketplace are sold via auction with a reserve price. After an NFT receives its first bid, a 24-hour countdown begins when other collectors can bid. The auction extends for another 15 minutes when bids come in 15 minutes before the auction closes.

To get started on Foundation as an artist, another community member has to invite you. When you receive an invite, you can use a MetaMask wallet to create an artist profile. Along with JPG or PNG files of your artwork, you need some ETH to post a listing to pay the fee to list on the Ethereum blockchain. (Market demand will change the cost each time.)

Foundation uploads your files to the InterPlanetary File System (IPFS), a protocol and peer-to-peer network for storing and sharing larger data across a distributed system. You then set a price in ETH and put it up for auction on Foundation Marketplace. You then receive 85 percent of the final sale price and a 10 percent royalty on future sales if sold on Foundation, OpenSea, or Rarible.

The Crypto.com NFT Platform

The Crypto.com NFT platform (https://crypto.com/nft) is a new addition to the family. Based in Hong Kong, the company runs its NFT marketplace as part of its exchange platform, which makes it easy to move funds to your wallet in order to buy NFTs.

Launched in 2021, this marketplace utilizes the Crypto.org Chain blockchain, which is a public, open source, and permissionless blockchain designed for payment, decentralized finance (DeFi), and NFTs.

The Crypto.com NFT platform launched with an exclusive deal with F1 Collectibles issued by the Aston Martin Cognizant Formula 1 racing team. Their first NFTs included race driver Sebastian Vettel and Lance Stroll in Aston Martin cars. Snoop Dogg has also launched several NFTs on Crypto.com.

As of this writing, Crypto.com charges no fees to artists or buyers. You can easily set up an account and add funds to your wallet. Artists can set up royalties up to 10 percent of the purchase price of resales. The platform accepts credit cards, and you don't need crypto to buy an NFT on this platform.

Chapter **13**

The Ten Most Expensive NFTs

In this chapter, you explore the most expensive NFTs of all time (at the time of writing) and the artists who created them. In today's world of rapidly developing technology, how artists create and share their work is also changing rapidly.

Because NFTs represent a new power shift that favors artists and collectors, learning about the most desirable NFTs and the work and thought that went into their creation is useful. This chapter helps you to gain a better understanding of the NFT phenomenon and the artists that are benefiting the most from this new trend. You can also gain a better understanding of the buyers who have been ready and willing to purchase this new type of art.

EVERYDAYS: THE FIRST 5000 DAYS

https://onlineonly.christies.com/s/beeple-first-5000-days/beeple-b-1981-1/112924

The most expensive NFT sold and bought to date is *EVERYDAYS: THE FIRST 5000 DAYS*, an artwork created by digital artist Mike Winkelmann, also known by his nickname, Beeple. This South Carolina-based graphical designer and motion artist has amassed over 1.8 million Instagram followers and collaborates with well-known brands such as Louis Vuitton and Nike. He has even worked with performing artists like Katy Perry and Childish Gambino.

Beginning in May 2007, Beeple began to create and post a new piece of art online every single day. *EVERYDAYS* is composed of the 5,000 digital pictures that Beeple posted online in a steady stream for each of those 5,000 days. This NFT is notable for being the first piece of purely NFT artwork to be sold by a major auction house — Christie's.

Beeple does more than just throw together 5,000 unrelated pictures to create *EVERYDAYS*. He creates a collage of recurring themes and color schemes, loosely organizing the pictures in chronological order to give the piece an aesthetic coherence. If you zoom in on the individual images inside the work, you can see how the artist evolves from basic drawings to 3D digital pictures. The piece includes many recurring themes, such as society's relationship with technology, wealth, and political turbulence in America.

The first digital picture Beeple created for the collage was a hand-drawn picture of his Uncle Jim, whom he nicknamed Uber Jay. His pieces later evolved to 3D works such as his drawing of Mike Pence with a fly on his head standing atop the White House. This is one of his more topical works of art, completed immediately after the 2020 vice presidential debate, and it was meant to serve as political commentary about the Trump administration. When viewed as a whole, the work cannot show the specific details of each individual image, but the JPEG version of the NFT is so large that the owner can zoom in on each piece to study them individually.

Beeple explains his evolution as an artist as becoming increasingly centered around reacting to current events. He has stated his desire to use 3D tools in his art to make comments on current events as they happen.

EVERYDAYs sold on March 11, 2021, for an astounding $69.3 million. Though bidding originally began at only $100, it grew to a bid of almost $30 million in the final few seconds of the auction. Then a flurry of last-minute bids prompted the auction to extend for two minutes, raising the final selling price to $69.3 million. According to the auction house that sold the NFT, this price makes the piece the third-highest auction price for a living artist, behind artists Jeff Koons and David Hockney.

Vignesh Sundaresan, also known as MetaKovan to the cryptocurrency community, bought the NFT. Sundaresan is the founder of the Metapurse NFT project, the largest NFT fund in the world. *EVERYDAYS* was created on the Ethereum blockchain, so Sundaresan will get a unique code existing on the Ethereum blockchain in addition to a gigantic JPEG of the NFT.

CryptoPunk #7523

`www.larvalabs.com/cryptopunks/details/7523`

The second most expensive NFT is *CryptoPunk #7523*, one of several Alien Punks created by Matt Hall and John Watkinson (founders of the studio Larva Labs). The *CryptoPunks* are a set of 10,000 pixel-art characters that were originally given out for free on the Ethereum blockchain when Larva Labs first made them in 2017. Inspiring the ERC-721 standard that powers almost all digital art and collectibles, *CryptoPunks* is one of the earliest examples of NFTs on Ethereum.

Known for their distinct characteristics, no two Punks are completely identical, and the blockchain has 10,000 Punks. The 9 Alien *CryptoPunks* are the rarest Punk types, compared to the 24 Apes, 88 Zombies, 3,840 Females, and 6,039 Males. Many *CryptoPunks* share similar accessories, such as pipes, sunglasses, caps, and eyepatches, but they mix and match the different accessories, skin colors, and types to create unique images.

All *CryptoPunks* are known for their aesthetic minimalism, as they're all 24-x-24-pixel, 8-bit-style NFTs. This particular CryptoPunk has blue green skin, a small gold earring on his right ear, and a brown beanie cap on his head — as well as a medical mask, which became symbolic of the COVID-19 pandemic despite not being intended that way when it was created. This is perhaps one of the biggest reasons it now exists as the highest-selling CryptoPunk NFT of all time.

Hall and Watkinson, who created *CryptoPunk #7523,* are creative technologists who have worked on almost every kind of software, from large-scale web infrastructure to genomics analysis software. In addition to the *CryptoPunks,* they've created the *Autoglyphs,* the first on-chain generative art on the Ethereum blockchain. (Here, *on-chain* means that the artwork itself is also stored on the blockchain.) They have worked with high-profile companies such as Google and Microsoft, and they've even created an app for Android, called AppChat, that makes a chat room for every app installed on a phone.

CryptoPunk #7523 was sold for $11.75 million on June 10, 2021, as part of Sotheby's online auction, "Natively Digital: A Curated NFT Sale." That this NFT sold for such a high price is partly because of the Punks' place at the heart of the NFT and crypto ecosystem. The *CryptoPunks* have taken on a unique symbol of online identity, giving whoever owns them access to one of the most sought-after NFTs in existence.

Israeli entrepreneur Shalom Meckenzie, the largest shareholder of digital sports betting company DraftKings, bought *CryptoPunk #7523.* Meckenzie also founded the gambling-technology provider SBTech in 2007, serving as its director until May 2014.

CryptoPunk #3100

www.larvalabs.com/cryptopunks/details/3100

The next NFT on the list is another *CryptoPunks,* this one titled *CryptoPunk #3100.* Many of the top-selling NFTs of all time are *CryptoPunks,* with half of the NFTs on this list in the *CryptoPunks* category. *CryptoPunk #3100* is another Alien CryptoPunk that features an Alien with blue green skin, no hair, and a blue-and-white striped headband. Though 406 of the *CryptoPunks* have headbands, none of them is exactly like this particular Alien CryptoPunk.

All *CryptoPunks* have been fetching relatively high prices, with the least expensive CryptoPunk currently for sale priced at slightly under $38,000. The average sale price for a CryptoPunk as of July 2021 was slightly under $200,000. Altogether, *CryptoPunks* sales have totaled more than $55 million.

CryptoPunk #3100 sold on March 11, 2021, for $7.58 million, or 4,200 ETH. It was sold on the Ethereum blockchain to a buyer who hasn't been named beyond their Etherscan account number. However, the owner of *CryptoPunk 3100* has recently begun offering the NFT for sale for 35,000 ETH, which is equal to $90.5 million. If a buyer were to acquire it for this price, it would make *CryptoPunk #3100* the most expensive NFT of all time.

CryptoPunk #7804

www.larvalabs.com/cryptopunks/details/7804

CryptoPunk #7804, the fourth most expensive NFT of all time, is another one of the nine Alien *CryptoPunks*. This Alien Punk is set apart by its dark gray cap and black sunglasses, but it's also smoking a brown pipe, similar to the *Sherlock Holmes*-style pipe. Even though 378 Punks come supplied with a pipe and 317 Punks come with sunglasses, this is the only Alien CryptoPunk to sport both items.

Dylan Field, Figma CEO, owned *CryptoPunk #7804* but sold it on March 10, 2021. When Field first acquired it, he told people he owned "the digital *Mona Lisa*." The low-resolution picture of a blue alien with a hat and a pipe was not originally deemed to have much value, but as *CryptoPunks* have become more and more valued in the NFT space, this particular NFT skyrocketed in value. Field was able to sell *CryptoPunk #7804* for $7.57 million.

Interestingly, he sold the NFT for 4,200 ETH, which is the same price that *CryptoPunk #3100* sold for. However, because of fluctuations in the price of ETH between the two sales, *CryptoPunk #7804* is valued at slightly less at the time of sale when translated into US dollars.

The new owner of *CryptoPunk #7804* isn't known beyond their Etherscan account number, but the account is listed as owning five other *CryptoPunks. CryptoPunk #7804* is listed for sale at the time of this writing at $383.86 million, which is significantly higher than any other NFT.

CROSSROAD

https://niftygateway.com/itemdetail/secondary/0x12f28e
2106ce8fd8464885b80ea865e98b465149/100010001

Fifth on the list of the most expensive NFTs sold thus far is another Beeple work, titled *CROSSROAD*. It was first sold before the 2020 election, and, unlike most NFTs, it was designed to change based on the outcome of the election. The NFT, as it stands now, is a 10-second video that depicts former President Donald Trump lying naked on the ground in a park, covered in words related to his campaign and portrayal in the media. In the video, pedestrians pass on the sidewalk as a bluebird resembling the Twitter mascot lands on Trump and tweets a picture of the clown emoji.

However, if Donald Trump had won the election, the NFT would have changed to feature him with a muscular body striding through flames and wearing a crown on his head. The first person to buy the NFT didn't know what the final artwork would look like, a point that Beeple intended as commentary on the uncertainty of the times. Although the initial buyer bought the NFT without knowing its final form, the latest buyer to purchase it — in February of 2021, months after the election had been decided — did know.

CROSSROAD was part of Beeple's first NFT sale on Nifty Gateway, the digital art platform and marketplace owned by the crypto exchange Gemini. Pablorfraile, the Twitter user who initially bought it, resold the piece — on February 22, 2021, for $6.6 million, more than 100 times its initial price — to an anonymous buyer with an account named Delphina Leucas. It is Beeple's second-most expensive NFT and the fifth-most expensive NFT of all time.

Like the individual digital pictures that comprise *EVERYDAYS*, *CROSSROAD* displays Beeple's signature political commentary in a provocative way. This NFT also exists on the Ethereum blockchain. At the time that the NFT was sold, it broke records by being the most expensive NFT of all time before *EVERYDAYS* beat it out a few weeks later.

OCEAN FRONT

```
https://niftygateway.com/itemdetail/primary/0x0151834a
6997f89eb8372ac54ac077d79bb4d1e0/7
```

The artist Beeple has yet another piece of art on the list of most expensive NFTs in the world. His work, *OCEAN FRONT*, sixth on the list, is a piece meant to speak to the challenge of climate change. The digital artwork features a tree growing out of a series of trailers and shipping containers that sit on a platform coming out of the ocean. In the image itself, the bright green foliage of the tree and the blue hues of the sky are contrasted with the dirty rust of the tanks underneath. The sky is also plagued by dark clouds and smog, with power lines traveling across the image and birds flying across in the background.

Beeple has stated that his piece represents what would happen if we were to do nothing to combat climate change. *OCEAN FRONT* was initially part of Beeple's *EVERYDAYS* series, posted with the caption, "Together we can solve this." It was auctioned on Nifty Gateway and received three successive bids from three Twitter users: @3fmusic, @BabyBelugaNFT, and Justin Sun, the founder and CEO of the TRON Foundation. Bidding started at $2.77 million, but Sun eventually purchased it for exactly $6 million.

Sun is known for his interest in the crypto space, having bid for many NFT artworks in the past. He also participated in the Christie's auction for *EVERYDAYS*, bidding $60 million before losing to the winning bid of $69 million. Sun stated that his intention in purchasing *OCEAN FRONT* was to help the TRON Foundation enter the NFT industry. He has plans to establish an NFT foundation soon and hire NFT artists and advisors to create more NFTs. Though the NFT was created on the Ethereum blockchain, Sun plans to permanently store the NFT on the TRON blockchain and the decentralized storage system BTFS.

In keeping with the climate change theme of *OCEAN FRONT*, Beeple committed to donating all $6 million of the proceeds to fight climate change. Beeple donated the proceeds to the Open Earth Foundation (https://openearth.org), a nonprofit organization that seeks to develop an open digital infrastructure designed to help combat climate change.

CryptoPunk #5217

www.larvalabs.com/cryptopunks/details/5217

CryptoPunk #5217 takes the spot of the seventh most expensive NFT of all time. This CryptoPunk, which is one of 24 Ape Punks, contains a gold chain and an orange knitted cap. Exactly 169 Punks have the gold chain accessory, and 419 Punks have the knitted cap accessory. *CryptoPunk #5217* likely sold for this price because of its rarity as one of the few Ape Punks for sale, which is the second rarest type of *CryptoPunks*, behind the Alien species.

Owner Snowfro sold *CryptoPunk #5217* on July 30, 2021, for $5.45 million, or 2,250 ETH, to an anonymous buyer, known only by their EtherScan account number. At the time of its sale, *CryptoPunk #5217* was the highest-selling NFT of the month. Like all *CryptoPunks* created by Larva Labs, *CryptoPunk #5217* was created on the Ethereum blockchain.

World Wide Web Source Code

www.sothebys.com/en/press/the-original-files-for-the-source-code-of-the-world-wide-web-sell-as-an-nft

The eighth NFT on the list takes you back to the beginning of the Internet, as this blockchain-based token represents the original World Wide Web Source Code. The inventor of the World Wide Web, Sir Tim Berners-Lee, announced that he would sell an NFT representing the original source code of the web in a Sotheby's auction.

The NFT itself depicts a series of white coding on a black background, a stark image that reduces the vast complexity of the Internet to its simplest roots. Though the NFT represents the web's source code, it's not the source code itself — the actual source code for the web is open source and in the public domain, so anyone who wants to can view it or copy it as they like.

An artistic way of representing the source code, presented with the title *This Changes Everything*, the NFT itself contains a package that includes an archive of the source code, a digital poster of the full code, a letter from Berners-Lee, and a half-hour video of the code being typed on a screen.

Funnily enough, the video in the NFT contains a coding error that may increase its value. Several of the characters written in the computing language C were mistakenly replaced with the computing language HTML, which only exists in the first place because of the creation of the web. Scott Burke of PleasrDAO, a decentralized investment collective that acquires NFTs, found the error.

Berners-Lee, also known as TimBL, is an English computer scientist widely credited with inventing the World Wide Web in 1989, based on an initial idea intended to help scientists share data with each other across the Internet. When he decided to release the source code for free, he ended up making the Web open to everyone. Since creating the World Wide Web, Berners-Lee has been knighted by Queen Elizabeth and named one of *Time* magazine's "100 Most Important People of the 20th Century."

This NFT was created on the Ethereum blockchain and sold on June 30, 2021, for $5.4 million to an anonymous buyer. On sale for a week at Sotheby's in New York, bidding began at $1,000, but a last-minute flurry of bids in the closing 15 minutes raised the price to $5.4 million.

Stay Free

https://foundation.app/@Snowden/stay-free-edward-snowden-2021-24437

The ninth most expensive NFT on the top ten list is *Stay Free*, an NFT created on the Ethereum blockchain and auctioned off by National Security Agency (NSA) whistleblower Edward Snowden. This work reproduces the 2015 Second Circuit Court of Appeals decision in ACLU v. Clapper, which ruled that the NSA was breaking the law with its mass surveillance program. The digital artwork overlays a portrait of Snowden on top of the array of documents detailing the court's decision. Platon, a British photographer who captured the photo of Snowden after an interview in Moscow, created the portrait. Snowden signed the work in the lower-right corner.

Snowden is notably responsible for one of the biggest leaks in US political history. He had been working at the NSA for four years as an employee of outside contractors when he discovered that the NSA was engaging in a mass surveillance program against the American public. He disclosed many top-secret documents to the public before fleeing the country. The revelations from the leak of these documents led to a cultural discussion about national security and the nature of individual privacy.

Snowden sold his NFT *Stay Free* for $5.4 million, or 2,224 ETH, on April 16, 2021. He did not keep the profits and instead donated them to the Freedom of the Press Foundation, of which he is the president. The Freedom of the Press Foundation is run by a board that includes notable figures such as whistleblower Daniel Ellsberg, writer Glenn Greenwald, and actor John Cusack.

Snowden has stated, "[E]merging applications of cryptography can play an important role in supporting our rights" in the Freedom of the Press Foundation statement. He believes that the auction of his NFT will help drive the development of privacy-protecting uses of encryption that can help safeguard the freedom of the press.

The winner of *Stay Free* is PleasrDAO, the same DAO ("decentralized autonomous organization") that caught the error in the World Wide Web source code NFT. PleasrDAO now owns *Stay Free* along with the NFT *x*y=k* by pplpleasr, a Taiwanese digital artist who recently joined the organization as an honorary member. Most of PleasrDAO's members have never met, and a few of them remain anonymous. They share a common philosophy, however, one which insists that the DAO be used to benefit society. They bought the Snowden NFT because they agree with Snowden's ideals around transparency for all, which they believe blockchains also help provide.

CryptoPunk #7252

www.larvalabs.com/cryptopunks/details/7252

Finally, the last NFT on the list, and the tenth most expensive NFT of all time, is *CryptoPunk* #7252, the fifth CryptoPunk and the only Zombie Punk to make the list. This CryptoPunk is one of 88 Zombie Punks, which is the third least-common type of Crypto-Punk available, behind the Alien *CryptoPunks* and the Ape *CryptoPunks*.

This green-skinned zombie has a brown chinstrap, a gold earring, and crazy red hair along with glowing red eyes. Of the 10,000 *CryptoPunks* and their accessories, 282 have chinstraps, 414 have crazy hair, and 2,459 have earrings.

This CryptoPunk may be last on the list of the top ten most expensive NFTs, but it's the most recent sale of all of them. Feng Bo bought *CryptoPunk* #7252 on August 24, 2021, for $5.33 million, or 1,600 ETH — more than twice what the previous buyer paid for it at \$2.53 million. Like all other *CryptoPunks*, this NFT was also created on the Ethereum blockchain.

Feng Bo, a Chinese investor, owns eight other *CryptoPunks*, all of which are human *CryptoPunks*. Feng Bo's investment is part of an overall trend among Chinese Internet investors entering the crypto economy by buying NFTs. Cai Wensheng, the founder of the Chinese technology company Meitu, is another Chinese investor, who recently bought another Punk titled *CryptoPunk #8236*. Meitu was one of the first publicly traded Chinese companies to invest heavily in cryptocurrencies, having purchased \$100 million in Ether and Bitcoin in early 2021.

Index

About the Authors

Tiana (T) and Seoyoung (Soy) have been friends for years and are excited to write their first book together as The Investor and The Professor. T and Soy both love food, wine, and interesting conversations, and this book has materialized at the intersection of their shared interests.

Dedication

This book is for our families — T's sisters, Alea and McKella, and Soy's parents, Mama Kim and Papa Kim, sister friend Celi, and fairy goddaughter Maddie. We are blessed to be loved, and we love you guys. ❤

Authors' Acknowledgments

This book would not have been possible without the ideas, work, and support of many talented people. Prefacing that order doesn't convey relative importance; we'd first like to thank the editorial team. Thank you to Steve Hayes (our executive editor) for making this happen, Paul Levesque and Nicole Sholly (our project editors) for keeping us on track, and Becky Whitney (our copy editor) for making sure we were intelligible and didn't make *For Dummies* fools of ourselves. We're also indebted to our technical editors — Philip Lee, Andre Nash, and Alex Cracraft — for their labor of love and expert attention to detail.

Tiana is also grateful to the open and welcoming blockchain-and-NFT community for the support and guidance they have provided her over the many years that she has been writing, building, and investing in the space. Specifically, her friends Scott Robinson, Casey Lawlor, Alyse Killeen, Jeremy Kandah, Anthony Shook, Tom Bollich, Bram Cohen, Brian Behlendorf, and others have helped shape her understanding of blockchain technology and the future of innovation. Tiana would also like to thank her research team — Joe Leonard and Will Rice.

Seoyoung is additionally grateful to Sanjiv Das, her longtime friend and colleague who indoctrinated her with techie ideology and brought her to Silicon Valley; Atulya Sarin, her friend and life coach, to whom she owes her academic career; and George Chacko, her friend and mentor who first suggested she create a FinTech course. All of Seoyoung's ideas and writings are a product of their expert guidance and thought leadership.

Publisher's Acknowledgments

Acquisitions Editor: Steve Hayes

Senior Project Editors:
Paul Levesque and Nicole Sholly

Copy Editor: Becky Whitney

Technical Editors: Philip Lee,
Andre Nash, and Alex Cracraft

Production Editor:
Mohammed Zafar Ali

Cover Image: © Oculo/Adobe Stock Photos